Hubert A. Allen, Jr.

Mount Hood
The Deep Blue Zone
Story of the 2006 Climbing Tragedy

Mount Hood
The Deep Blue Zone
Story of the 2006 Climbing Tragedy

By Hubert A. Allen, Jr.

First Edition, 2009
Published by:
Hubert Allen and Associates
720-25 Tramway Lane, NE
Albuquerque, New Mexico 87122   USA

Publisher's Cataloging-in-Publication
Allen, Hubert A.
        Mount Hood : the deep blue zone : story of the 2006
        climbing tragedy / by Hubert A. Allen. -- 1st ed.
        p. cm.
        Includes bibliographical references.
        ISBN-13: 978-0-9792740-4-6
        ISBN-10: 0-9792740-4-4

        1. Mountaineering accidents--Oregon--Hood, Mount.
I. Title.

GV199.42.H64A45 2007   796.522'09795
                                     QBI07-600150

Dedication

To all men and women
who provide or coordinate Search and Rescue worldwide
Thank You

Disclaimer

The author partly relied on the vast amount of reporting which occurred during the Mount Hood Search and Rescue effort of December 2006 to write this book. A trip to Mount Hood in February 2007 was used to trace the climbers last day in contact with other people on the mountain. Interviews with several of the key players in the search were conducted at this time. The author brought to the meetings a set of weather estimates for the first days of the climb at approximately 11,000 feet on Mount Hood and contributed these tables to the on-going investigation(s) by the various agencies and groups involved in the search and rescue effort. None of these reports had been finalized by the February 2007 trip to Mount Hood. Narrative of the climber's journey was reconstructed from all the available evidence, direct and indirect and experiential. Some of this book is conjecture but it is based on the best available facts and evidence mixed with the author's own winter climbing experiences. The contents of this book may change and be up-dated as investigations are completed and more evidence is released to the public. However, this book is sold as is and as such is non returnable in any venue. In the end, the author takes full responsibility for the contents of this book and has made every effort to put forth the truth.

> Hubert A. Allen, Jr.
> March 1, 2007

Revisions

This version includes results of an August 2007 research trip to Mount Hood during which the greatest media myth of this incident was shattered, and the truth revealed - August 20, 2007.

Contents

Introduction

Between earth and heaven lie the mountain summits. Snow shoeing up the last bendy hill, I can smell the wood smoke still drifting out a cooling stove pipe of the Tilly Jane warming hut. It is the very same hut three climbers Kelly James, Brian Hall, and Jerry "Nikko" Cooke spent their last night among fellow humans. By accounts the three were entertaining, polite and generous. Signing the hut register the night before their ill-fated climb they mention how the warmth of the fireplace caused them to change plans. Instead of continuing up Mount Hood to bivouac in a snow cave, the seduction of Tilly Jane led them to sleep here instead. And surely they had that Thursday afternoon to catch-up among themselves and psyche up for the North Face climb the next day. Sitting in the Tilly Jane warming hut writing, I now know that each hour they sat cheerily in the hut was one lost on the North Face the next day - at the time it was over-looked by the climbers as to the true cost of this affair with Tilly Jane. This book is the story of those three men and their epic attempt on Mount Hood that December in 2006. Facts are piecemeal, evidence scarce but the reality of the outcome undisputed. If we as fellow climbers, indeed as fellow humans, can walk away with even one lesson learned it will have been worth writing.

Hubert A. Allen, Jr.
The Tilly Jane warming Hut
Northside, Mount Hood, Oregon, USA
February 3, 2007

Mount Hood: The Deep Blue Zone

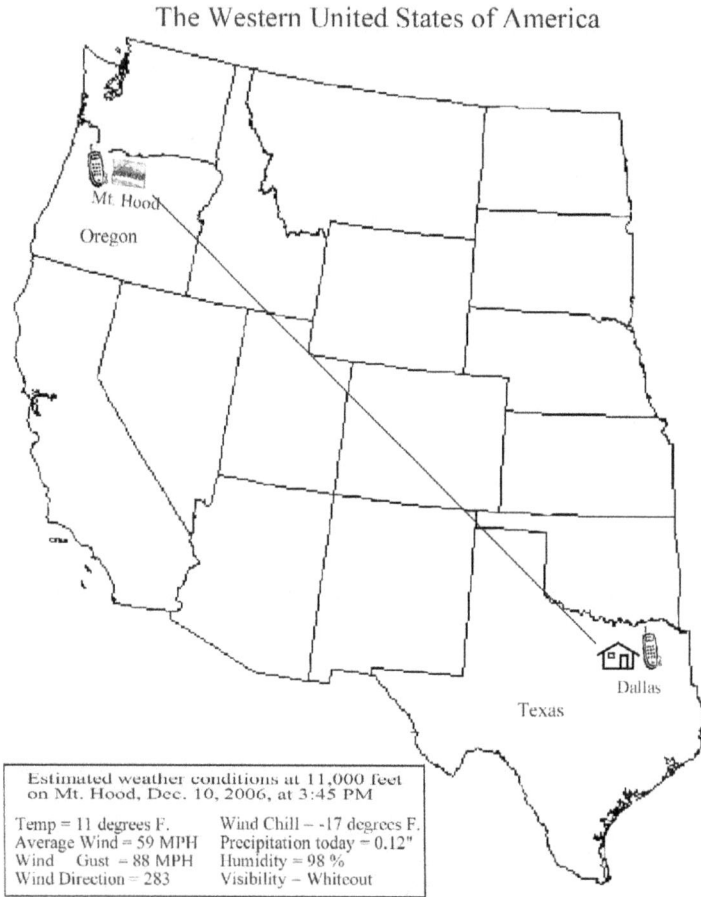

The Western United States of America

Mt. Hood

Oregon

Dallas

Texas

Estimated weather conditions at 11,000 feet
on Mt. Hood, Dec. 10, 2006, at 3:45 PM

Temp = 11 degrees F.   Wind Chill = -17 degrees F.
Average Wind = 59 MPH   Precipitation today = 0.12"
Wind   Gust = 88 MPH   Humidity = 98 %
Wind Direction = 283   Visibility = Whiteout

Map 1: A cell phone call from climber Kelly James in a snow cave high
on Oregon's 11,239 foot tall Mount Hook set off the search and rescue.

A Cell Phone Call

(Sunday - December 10, 2006)

At the end of the first Sunday night, December 10th 2006, headline news was brewing across America about a team of climbers trapped on a wintry Mount Hood, in Oregon. The primary source of this news was a remarkable cell phone call from somewhere high on Mount Hood to family members in Dallas, Texas. It was not a mere partial exchange but an actual conversation between loved ones.

Stuck on the frozen mountainside, a husband spoke to his wife via cell phone. She could tell by the sound of his voice that he was in trouble. This was no casual check-in, nor was it a celebratory call from a balmy summit. Karen knew from the tone of her husband Kelly's voice that this was an extremely serious call.

After all, she knew Kelly had been mountain climbing for 25 years. He was a seasoned mountaineer who had climbed in South America, on Mount McKinley in Alaska, and on other Cascade climbs. In fact, their relationship, his second marriage, had been all about mountains. He had proposed marriage to her while they were on top of Mount Rainier, in Washington state and she had accepted. They planned a fiftieth wedding anniversary back on top of Mount Rainier.

This cell phone call was unlike any they had ever had. He told her that he was stuck high on Mount Hood in a snow cave with a storm blasting outside. He was cold, wet, weak and alone. He had only half an orange to eat. There was no stove roaring in the background. His two climbing companions had left for rescue the day before.

Immediately understanding the magnitude of her husband's situation, for she had been with him on dozens of mountain adventures and was an insider, she knew it was her duty to stand strong - as Kelly was on the faint, crackly cell phone connection.

The call only lasted four precious minutes. In which Kelly could hardly provide the details necessary to be easily located. Then it was over. There was no success in reconnecting but the very fact that Kelly had been speaking on the end of his cell phone from somewhere on Mount Hood was a reassurance full of clues.

Karen immediately called the authorities. For background, she could only tell them that her husband and his two companions had planned on leaving their car at the base of the north side of Mount Hood on Thursday, December 7th, 2006. This being Sunday, the fourth day, she was expecting a joyous call from the summit of Mount Hood itself, with a swaggering husband on the line, talking about the next adventure. But that was not the call she got.

The North Face Route on Mount Hood. (Photo Credit: The Author)

The Climbing Plan
(Summer 2006 - December 7, 2006)

The plan for climbing Mount Hood sprang forward at the moment these three climbers reached the summit of Mount Rainier the prior summer. It was on that trip that Jerry "Nikko" Cooke first met up with Kelly James and Brian Hall, the climbing team from Dallas, Texas. An instant friendship grew between the men while on Mount Rainier and they wanted to lock-in an adventure for the trio to attempt.

The detailed plan for the Mount Hood climb then evolved over the course of the next several months. By late November they had a climbing plan and the airline tickets to make it happen in early December.

It was a logical plan, a brilliant-sounding plan, a magnificent plan as it stood on paper. Well, paper was old fashioned, and one of the climbers, Jerry, in Brooklyn, New York, was not an old fashioned 36 year old. Jerry posted a version of the climbing plan in November 2006 on an Internet blog. In this plan, the North Face climb was going to take 24-36 hours total to complete the round-trip, car-to-car. As the team saw it, this was going to be a lightning fast ascent, exceedingly fast, and light on gear and supplies. It was a high-risk venture, no doubt. But they were strong enough climbers to be able to do this relatively untechnical ice face, given just the Grade III, or half-day climb rating, in one popular climbing guide.

But in early winter? On an 11,239 foot mountain in the northern reaches of America? Yes, it could be done, there was a logic behind the strategy. Early winter could provide good conditions for climbing on the more difficult North Face of Mount Hood.

In early December, technically before winter actually starts, the dangerous shedding of ice and rock would cease. The longer nights and freezing conditions would begin to cement all of natures elements into one solid mass. Mount Hood might actually come into an optimal condition at this time of year. When the hazardous summit cornices, which grow from nothing to huge, threatening over-hangs of snow and ice during the summer and fall, are less likely to be threatening.

Then climbing the North Face of Mount Hood, perched menacingly above the Eliot Glacier, might be done at its absolute fastest. Faster and, perhaps, safer than in summer because in optimal conditions the icy would be like plastic, and there would be less dodging a continuous hail of snow, ice and rock.

Faster is often safer in the mountains. The less time one spent at higher elevations, the better off the body would be. Spend a lot of time at elevation and there was more chance for the body to rebel; headaches, loss of appetite, and heaven forbid, pulmonary edema - drowning in one's own fluids as they fill up the lungs, suffocating the climber.

Conceivable, if one could climb Mount Hood fast enough, on the optimal snow/ice medium, in good weather, a team might use an eight-hour period of sunlight to go from a crude bivouac, as close to the start of the serious climbing as possible, to the 11,239 foot summit and then back down to the same starting point, or lower, possibly as far down as the Tilly Jane warming hut at 5,837 feet. This would require a perfect day of climbing, in perfect weather, with each man at the top of his game. Going light and fast in best conditions - it could definitely be done in early December.

There was a certain climber-logic at play, 'If you can climb up a hard route fast, you can certainly descend an easy route even faster.' It all added up to a Climbing Plan for a lightning fast 24-36 hours on Mount Hood, from base to summit and back, and a North Face bagged in winter. One, maybe two nights out before returning to the car.

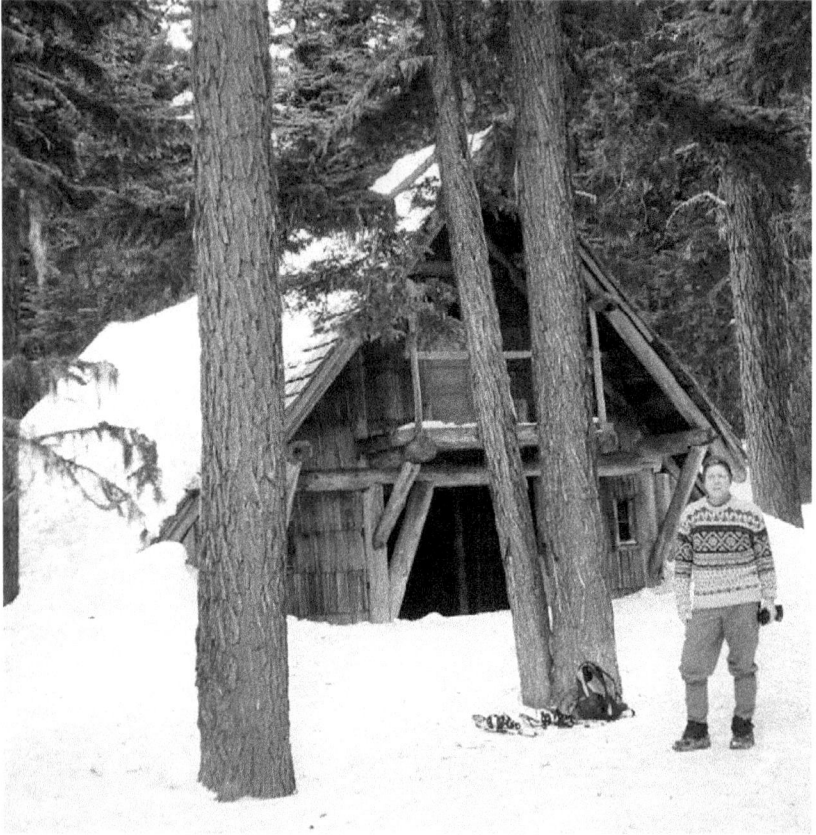

Climber Jon Williams at the Tilly Jane warming hut, February 3, 2007. The size and comforts of the hut are more than one expects on the north side of Mount Hood. (Photo Credit: The Author)

Tilly Jane Warming Hut
(Climber's Day -1 - Thursday - December 7, 2006)

On the road to the base of Mount Hood, Kelly, Brian and Jerry must have had ten tons of catching up to do between them. Even though Kelly and Brian were both from the Dallas area, their lives were busy and they didn't have time to visit very often. Jerry was from Brooklyn, New York. He had sent a flood of e-mails and many phone calls to his friends in Texas to get this adventure organized.

After all, the three had been planning the trip since last summer, when they conceived the plan on top of Mount Rainier. That summer day was just perfect, as had been the entire Rainier climb. A winter ascent of Mount Hood's North Face was a bold idea in the first place. But here they were, the three climbing buddies, with over 30 years of climbing experience between them.

Driving eastward in darkness, out Interstate 84, they exit at the small hamlet of Hood River and turn south on Route 35 just as day's first light appears. There, directly in front of them, rises the awesome stature of Mount Hood, the steep white cone of their destiny. They must have been deeply happy. They may not have seen it but a government weather map for the day was, if anything, reassuring.

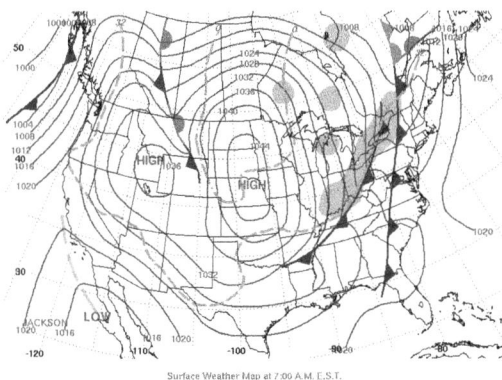

Surface Weather Map at 7:00 A.M. E.S.T.

About fifteen miles south they stop at the Hood River Ranger Station. But they are there even earlier than the first hardy Forest Service employee. The Ranger Station is open and staffed at 7:30am on weekdays. They slip a short note in a winter wood box and continue the last few miles to the snow park near the Cooper Spur ski and snow boarding area at the Tilly Jane trailhead, just a few minutes drive further up the mountain.

Kelly had heard about this Tilly Jane warming hut, and as the total distance to the summit was a bit more than six miles, it sure seemed the Tilly Jane at 2.7 miles, and about 1,900 feet of elevation gain, was a good start.

On the bulletin board at the trailhead was a list of winter equipment. And the trail itself was packed down, even though there had been quite a lot of fresh snow the prior two weeks. It looked packed enough that they decided to leave the rented snowshoes in the car. Less weight, going fast and light. They leave a gallon of fuel for the cooking stove in the car for their return. As the three good friends walk away from the car about 8am, they follow an easy trail upwards through the forest. The note left on the car, written on a piece of brown paper bag, said:

> "We are a party of three attempting the North Face. Ranger station was closed so we couldn't buy a parking permit. We plan to sleep 12/7 on route and descend south side on Friday. We will retrieve truck Saturday afternoon. (35 will be open.) DO NOT TOW! In emergency storm we will descend Cooper Spur and have food and fuel in truck. We will be happy to pay for permit Saturday. Thanks, Jerry Cooke."

The three men must have enjoyed the walk up from the car to the Tilly Jane warming hut. The weather is excellent, just above freezing as they hit the trail and warming into the forties during the afternoon. The distance of 2.7 miles is modest, and the trail in condition from other winter enthusiasts - and Oregon has many. The snow depth at 5,250 feet is five feet.

18

Seeing the substantial A-frame Tilly Jane warming hut after rounding the last bend and coming up the hill was a pleasant surprise. With the early start, they reach the hut between 10am and 11am.

Walking through the always open entranceway, the men encounter an anteroom with sawdust and wood chip flooring. To one side is the outhouse, a small wooden room with toilet paper available. Opening the door into the hut itself one is struck with the good size of the structure and the large stove and a couple of picnic tables. The walls have information and a guest book. It is a warm and cheerful hut. The fire is often simmering, dying out from the early morning users. A loft above the main room is completely empty of furniture, available for the night's lodgers.

Tilly Jane warming hut, February 3, 2007. (Photo Credit: The Author)

The afternoon is warm. The decision is made to stay at the hut and try and wake up at 3am to begin the climb. Are they aware of another, simpler hut called the Copper Spur Shelter about 1.1 miles further up, another 800 feet higher in elevation on the Cooper Spur? With clear skies the moon is only four days from being full, reflecting off snow the 3am start sounds plausible. Sleeping in the simple but warm hut at 5,837 feet the climbers are elated. Everything is going well. Before going to sleep the team writes a note in the log book of the Tilly Jane warming hut:

> "12/7/6, Thanks for your hard work on this great Shelter. We did not plan on staying, but the warmth of the fire changed our minds. We climb as a group of 3 and we left a $20 bill. We will leave tomorrow for the North Face! Wish us luck! Nikko, B. Hall, Krazy Kelly."

Register and pay box at the Tilly Jane warming hut, February 3, 2007. (Photo Credit: The Author)

They cache much of the gear they are not wearing or do not need for the technical climb adjacent to the hut. They carefully place the treasure trove of equipment, food and clothing under a board, thinking they will be back in 24 to 36 hours.

The North Face Climb
(Climber's Day -2 - Friday - December 8, 2006)

When this team of three men say good-bye to the Tilly Jane warming hut, they are saying good-bye to all of humanity's accouterments and stepping forward into the harsh primitive reality of a big mountain in winter. It is not, however, a 3am departure. Even with moonlight, finding the gully, which is the shortest way up to the North Face, is tricky if you have never been there before. A maze of tracks surrounds the Tilly Jane even in winter and none of the climbers have ever been anywhere on Mount Hood before. They are still below tree line, and just a little bit of light would make all the difference.

Leaving behind the lovely little building, perhaps between 6 and 7am, and having spent a wonderful night at America's oldest high altitude ski cabin, they are aiming higher than even trees venture, above the timber line, towards the 11,239 foot summit of Mount Hood.

The weather breaks nicely this climbing day. The sun rises at 7:38am, the temperature at the Hut hovers around 37°F. There is a light wind all morning, averaging between six and 10mph at this lower elevation. But, even here there are occasional wind gusts to 26mph. There would be no precipitation at all this day. It is a glorious day to be climbing Mount Hood in winter. Besides, it technically is not even winter for another two weeks. That is part of the brilliance of the plan, call it a winter ascent even if technically that was a bit of cheating.

There is, unfortunately, one 'rub' as Shakespeare put it, eating at the team. The hike the day before up to the Tilly Jane warming hut had been on well-beaten snow-covered ground making it an easy trek. Today it is a completely different situation. Almost as soon as they leave the hut, they find themselves post-holing through the snow. Their feet breaking through the crusty snow surface, down two feet or more, and plant like a tree trunk. Each man struggles to keep balance and then pulls one foot out to make the next uncertain step.

23

The lead man is breaking trail and expending a lot of energy, psychological as well as physical - it is a draining task. The second and third man also work hard just to match their leader's tracks. Every so often, Kelly, Brian and Jerry trade positions, taking turns breaking trail. The going is much slower than they expected.

Now the decision to leave the snow shoes in the car comes up. They should have brought them. That is quickly becoming painfully, energy-draining, time-consumingly obvious to the three climbers. But they press on now able to see the glaciers and North Face above them. This energy burn is compounding the trouble with the mathematics of an elevation gain of nearly 5,400 feet from the Tilly Jane hut to the summit of Mount Hood, the day's objective.

The higher the climbers go, the lower the temperature goes. Rule of thumb is to subtract 3.7° F. for every 1,000 feet of elevation gain. Winds, less easy to extrapolate, can easily be between 20mph and 30 mph higher near Mount Hood's 11,239 foot summit than at a measly 5,837 feet of the Tilly Jane warming Hut.

A small front is moving in from the Southwest, with light precipitation in the forecast. The temperature peaks about 11am, and begins a steady decline.

The climbers work their way up to the mighty North Face itself, crossing Eliot Glacier. They are roped as they cross the glacier. On some of the steepening terrain they can climb simultaneously. However, the steepness soon demands the safety of belay anchors, and belaying the leader, rope length after rope length on steep ice. Finally they are high on the couloirs, the crux area of the North Face Route. It is unclear what the climbing conditions are when they finally get to this serious 50°- 60° angle climbing on snow and ice terrain but the climbers decide to press onto the crux.

The terrain is no longer familiar to the human being. Everything is tilted at a ridiculous angle. Everyone is using their ice tools and crampons like nails to bite into the icy mountain. The ice axe and smaller ice hammer, along with the front-points of the crampons, are now functioning at their highest level. The climbing progresses in technical fashion, which is why they came. This is the excitement. The controlled, climbing thrill.

It's different than what Jerry practiced on while climbing the Frankenstein Cliffs, in Crawford Notch, in northern New Hampshire in winter. Those ice cliffs were frozen waterfalls which produced brittle but firm ice anywhere from 30° to 90° or beyond. The ice and snow on Mount Hood is much more plastic and the picks go in deeply. Jerry used to go up to New Hampshire and hire a guide to improve his climbing, and he could easily climb this stuff. Brian had been Kelly's climbing partner for almost six years, and they knew each other's capabilities.

Each climber could have led pitches up the 2,500 foot North Face, and swinging leads between men is the tradition. Then again, Kelly James was by far the most experienced of the three. Twenty-five years of climbing experiences. He may have done the lion's share of leading. By mid afternoon they would be near the end of the technical difficulties and near the top of the North Face.

By the time the climbers approach the 10,000 foot elevation, ambient air temperature alone does not tell the story. It is about 30° F. at 1pm. Average wind estimated to be 33 mph with a gust up to 52 mph. The combined Wind Chill Factor for the climbers is now 14° F. They might have gleaned some protection due to the topography of the face, let us hope so.

The last photograph on their camera is a classic shot of a climber on this serious part of the face, probably above 10,000 feet. Brian wore a layer of yellow. At the moment everything appears in working order. Yet, there is a nagging fear in seeing the shadows, deep shadows, sometime between 2pm and 3pm and still 1,000 vertical feet to go.

Then something happens. Probably between 3pm and 4pm, something bad happens. Winds are howling at 38 mph. Blowing snow dramatically cuts visibility. Each man has just about run out of steam. Suddenly chaos ensues. Motion. Someone takes a fall, and the others catch him, perhaps tethered to a classic 'Y-shaped' anchor.

Someone has his legs scraped along the ice leaving abrasions. The others hold him. There is a pregnant moment where all three men are tightly bound by the rope holding them and a taught anchor.

Right where the two anchored climbers sit, they begin to build a trivial belay stance into a deeper snow platform. Sunset is approaching. They dig out a much more substantial snow platform than for a quick stop, where only half an hour is spent. This snow platform is deep enough to cut the wind, but not so deep as to be a snow cave with complete protection for an over-night bivouac.

They are trying to get a moment's break from the elements to allow the shock of the incident to wear off, to assess where each man is physically and psychologically. To regain a semblance of equilibrium for the team.

At 4pm the temperature is around 20° F, average winds at 39 mph with a gust at 49 mph. The wind chill factor brings the effective temperature down to -1° F for the climbers near the 11,000 foot level. At 4:27pm the sun will set.

On the snow platform things are getting desperate. The weather is caving in. Exhaustion and hypothermia stalk the climbers. The wind is howling, mocking, killing. What can we do?

At this time, if not sooner, the disadvantage of going light is also becoming obvious. They are in the beginning stages of hypothermia. They did have a couple of bivy sacks, light shells in which clothing or a sleeping bag can be contained to hold heat, with the sack protecting from water and acting as a buffer against the cold ground.

As they try to discuss the options, they can barely hear the words let loose just six inches away from each other because of the wind. The sun has long been invisible from this place on the North Face. What to do? They must act.

Up or down?

It's not much further, maybe less than three hundred feet to get to what must be the summit area. And it looks fairly easy going from the snow platform. Once off the North Face they can either immediately cut back down to get onto the Cooper Spur as the emergency exit. Or, they can cross over the summit plateau and descend via the south side. They had identified both possibilities in their note left on their car at the Tilly Jane trailhead.

26

Earlier in the day, Kelly, Brian and Nikko had walked up the climber's trail on the glacial moraine, in clear weather. From the Cooper Spur shelter they marched to a position just below the Cooper Spur Snowfield, with the North Face to the right and the crumbly maze of the East Face around to the left of the Cooper Spur. The Cooper Spur Route was the logical descent route. Each man has his mental map of this escape. This was the bail route!

Meanwhile someone was in no shape to even be using ice axes and needs to be roped in between the other two. The rope is decisively cut - showing a clear mark made intentionally by the climbers. Some rope is left on the floor of the snow platform This technique of 'short-roping' gives them more stability in the vile winds which threaten to quite literally blow them off the mountain.

Given, an accident may have just occurred, and yet the climbers have pulled themselves into motion again. Two ice hammers are left on the floor of this icy platform as the threesome climb out and off the North Face.

They begin climbing simultaneously, giving the man in the middle maximum support and steadying him in the face of horrific winds and white-out conditions, leaving three sets of parallel tracks, running up from the snow platform to the summit area.

There is no time or energy to go for the actual summit, that means topping out and going to the right. They need the shortest, fasted descent route possible and that is the Cooper Spur Route in reverse. It means topping out on the summit area and going left. Then try to find a passage down to the lower Cooper Spur Route and off the highest elevations. They had a cache of food and gear back at the Tilly Jane hut, tucked safely under a board next to the hut.

Moving together the trio painfully covers the remaining few hundred feet to break free of the North Face. Here the triad has a greater strength. But, the cost of all the day's mis-timings is that when they reach the summit area it is utterly dark and inhuman conditions prevail. So dark, windy and torturous is the blowing snow that movement for the three is painfully slow. Plans for a rational descent simply became un-executable.

The Deep Blue Zone
(Climber's Day -2 - Friday - December 8, 2006 - Evening)

At 4pm on Friday, at the Meadows ski area weather station at 6,600 feet, the average hourly wind speed was a modest 9mph, with gusts to 19mph. Temperature recorded at 37° F. It sounds somewhat harmless. Now throw in a fudge factor for estimating conditions four thousand feet higher on Mount Hood. Drop the temperature by 3.7° F. for every 1,000 feet of elevation gained, a total of about 15° F cooler at 11,239 feet at the summit. Winds are even more cruelly extrapolated, and in stormy conditions can add 30 mph for those in the higher elevations.

That means the steady wind the climbers are fighting, with every move, with every part of their bodies, is blowing 39mph with gusts up to 49 mph lashing them on that icy summit. The Wind Chill Factor brings the temperature down to -1° F. high on Mount Hood. Just as the sun is setting in a haze of color, the three climbers suddenly find themselves entering conditions of devastatingly extreme cold and wind, so piercing that it quickly challenges the very premise of human life, a place called the Deep Blue Zone.

In the Deep Blue Zone effective cold is subzero and winds are unrelenting. Wind is the defining force in the Deep Blue Zone. High winds lower the effect of temperature from what looks reasonable to the much colder Wind Chill value, which is the reality the climbers are facing. Wind stirs up existing snow and visibility is reduced, perhaps to within a body length. Even the act of looking is difficult, painful and usually not very helpful. You are virtually blinded.

No part of the human being is immune to this bombardment of wind and cold, not even the mind. As the strength of the body is sucked away, the mind begins its defense by pulling in as well. There is a tempting serenity to being enveloped by The Deep Blue Zone.

But Kelly, Brian and Jerry don't give in. They reach the summit area of Mount Hood, and now they only have to get back down via a reversal of the Cooper Spur Route. But it is dark, abysmally dark, and with the winds a spray of small, icy particles find their way into everything. They continue to be short-roped and try to locate the precise side of the mountain top they have to descend to reverse the Cooper Spur Route. They have to get off the windswept summit and back down to any possible shelter on the face below. Selecting a descent off the face in these conditions is virtually impossible, but down a side of Mount Hood they traveled, roped closely together, in the dead of night. Each man is working feverishly, knowing that they are now in survival mode. This was no game, no realization of a grand strategy, this is a pure fight for survival.

But there they are, back on a difficult face of Mount Hood, in the dark, on a stance being swept by spindle and constant, punishing winds and gusts that can easily pull an unanchored man off the mountain and down the 2,500 foot face. They fight this same battle for the equivalent of one or two more rope lengths and then they are, literally, at the end of their tether. Unanimously, or, perhaps, it was the decision of one coherent man, at this belay stance they begin digging into the side of the mountain. There may be some protection from the worst winds at this spot.

Once the decision is made, each man might feel a sense of relief, a feeling that this decision is the one thing they could do to survive. By now they each know that continuing down the face at night, in these conditions, would fail. If they want to survive the night they have to dig. So they immediately switched energies into digging the snow cave.

This kind of digging is not the fun adventure in the backyard during the first winter storm. No, this is digging because your very life depends on scratching out this snow cave, now, and as fast as you can. They have one shovel. Who will dig with that? Who will use their ice axe to scrape away the ice? The digging scene has a surreal quality to it. A few drained humans frantically scratching out a den at nearly 11,000 feet above sea level during a terrific wind storm.

When finally they dig deep enough for all three men to fit inside, several hours have passed and it is well into the night. Amazingly, they have pulled themselves out of the killer wind. Against all odds, they secure themselves a foothold high on Mount Hood; away from the wind but each man badly hypothermic and dehydrated with hands dangerously close to becoming frost-bitten, and feet numb as logs.

Inside the cocoon of the snow cave the men actively work to warm themselves up. The struggle to dig the cave has brought each man near to his limit. Penetrating cold, aggravated by the very act of digging in snow and ice, has taken a toll on hands, feet, all extremities. There is a working stove with fuel for the night but no more. It takes a while for the temperature in the snow cave to warm, but fairly soon it may have risen to near-freezing or higher. Slowly, the pins and needles feeling of frost nipped flesh coming back to life returns to the climbers. Eventually, having halted a creeping hypothermia, at least to a steady state, they doze through the black night.

Yes, they are all three alive; the buddies Kelly, Brian and Jerry. They still have each other. But outside the small sheltered snow cave the winds howl until midnight while the temperatures trended colder and colder. The three men have made their first venture in the realm of the Deep Blue Zone. In the 24 hours which ended with the men surviving in a snow cave 300 feet below the summit of Mount Hood, exactly zero precipitation fell on the mountain. In the Deep Blue Zone you don't need precipitation, its all about the wind and cold.

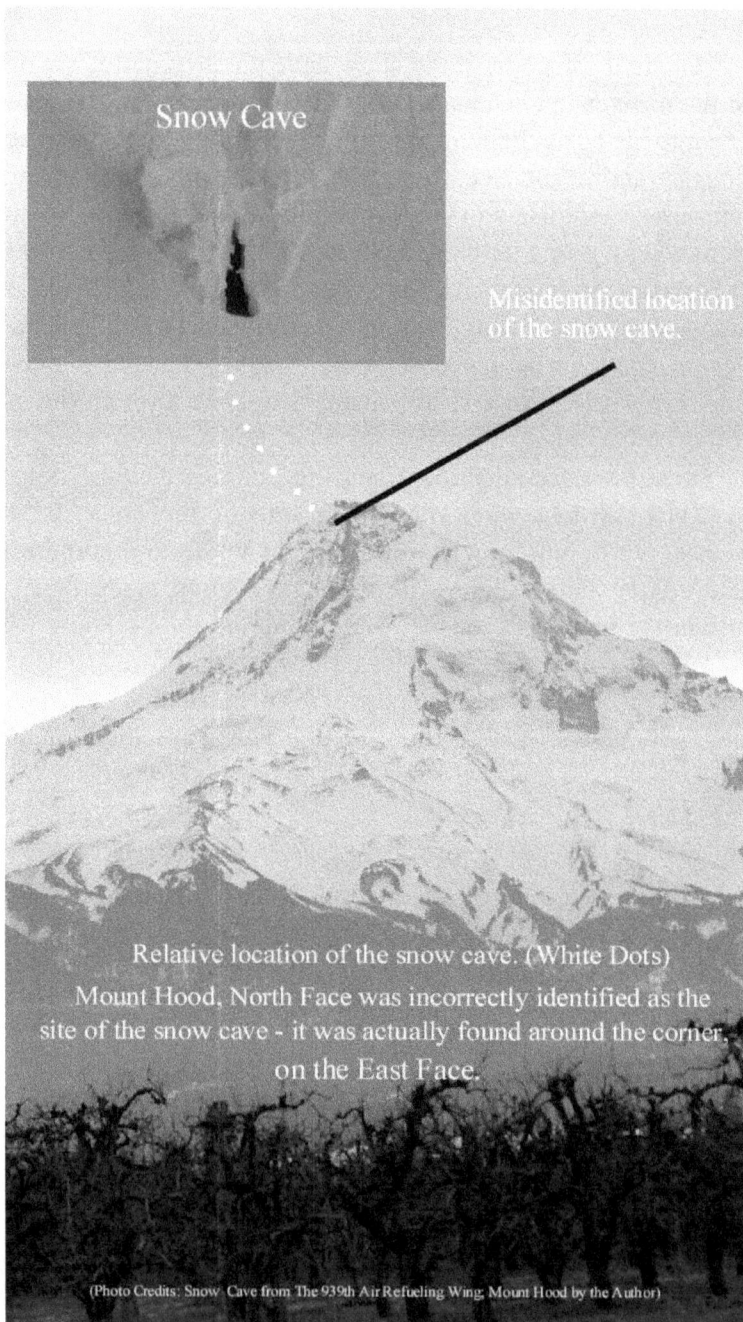

Snow Cave

Misidentified location of the snow cave.

Relative location of the snow cave. (White Dots)
Mount Hood, North Face was incorrectly identified as the site of the snow cave - it was actually found around the corner, on the East Face.

(Photo Credits: Snow Cave from The 939th Air Refueling Wing; Mount Hood by the Author)

The Snow Cave

(Climber's Day -3 - Saturday - December 9, 2006)

Saturday's first light brought even higher winds than they struggled against the previous night. Much lower on the mountain, at 6,600 feet, they blew unmercifully all morning at speeds over 22mph and gusts to 51mph, with day time temperatures having dipped to around 30° F. That is fact.

Meteorological extrapolation estimates that what the climber's are experiencing this morning is more like steady winds at 52mph and gusts to 81mph. Temperatures in the teens. Wind chill at -14° F. On top of this it starts to snow. We do not know exactly how much snow fell on the mountain heights, but down at 5,250 feet they recorded 0.51 inches of rain from 4am to 9am. Thus, morning find the men still pinned down in this Deep Blue Zone.

Here and now there was a discussion of the utmost gravity. Not only would they be assessing the difficulty of their position on the mountain, a snow cave at approximately 11,000 feet above sea level in dreadful conditions, but each man would have to assess himself. What was the cost of Mount Hood's wintry summit been on the body of each man? The outcome of this discussion is known through the facts and decisions made by the climbers.

Kelly is the oldest man in the group at age 48. Brian and Jerry are ages 37 and 36, respectively. All men are physically fit and trained for the trip. There are no physical slouches in the team. Nonetheless, the toll of the preceding day on Kelly was such that he knew he could not physically make the descent off the mountain. Exhaustion, cramping, dehydration, little food - every little trouble added up to a final, and very profound decision, for Kelly James to stay holed up in the snow cave while his two companions, Brian and Jerry together went for help.

For Jerry Cooke, the newest member of the triad, having met Kelly and Brian just the previous summer, being in on the rescue side of a climbing accident had happened before. In July 2005 he was out for his third attempt at climbing Mount Rainier with a partner, David

Valdes. They were on the Emmons Glacier when Valdes suddenly fell into a crevasse and down ten feet, and then another plunge of ten feet more and another five feet again before Jerry self-arrested, got his footing, held his ground, and saved both himself and his partner from a bad fall. Luckily, two other climbers were near-by and they quickly gorilla-hauled the two hapless climbers out of the jaws of an icy hole. Jerry would muster that same strength to get rescue for Kelly.

Unfortunately, this is much more serious. The average winds and gusts are unmerciful. The terrain is again the steep 50° to 60° angle. Snow falls from 4am for five straight hours. With time already drifting powerlessly away from the climbers, Brian and Jerry quickly have to make a final departure from Kelly when anything resembling a tiny moderation of conditions is detected.

This is when Brian and Jerry leave Kelly in the snow cave and go for rescue, sometime late in the morning or early on Saturday afternoon amid the spindrift avalanches, and whiteout conditions. It's impossible to see the forest through the trees and any distance, anywhere.

There are foot tracks leading off in several directions from the snow cave, suggesting that the first work out of the cave was some reconnaissance of the immediate area. However, two sets of tracks then appear to go downslope a ways, to where a rocky cliff cuts off easy access. Brian and Jerry are forced to explore the edges of this abyss.

At high noon average winds blow at 54 mph and gust to 78 mph. A human can barely stand in winds of 35 mph on flat ground. Even roped and on belay it was impossible to be in control of one's motion from second to eternal second. There were more than 2,000 feet of a steep Mount Hood Face on the downside of that cliff.

This is the best case scenario for our three climbers: one alive in a snow caves and the other two searching a way down a treacherous face of Mount Hood - 36 hours after leaving the Tilly Jane warming hut. Still alive, breathing, thinking, and praying. There was still hope at this moment.

Alone

(Climber's Day - 4 - Sunday - December 10, 2006)

Kelly James woke up on Sunday morning in a snow cave by himself to the roar of fifty mile an hour winds and bitter cold. It was white-out conditions. The Deep Blue Zone had descended like an impenetrable wall. Brian and Jerry had left the day before. How many hours had it been since they left? At least the night had passed in relative calm. But outside the snow cave entrance he could see and hear the horrific condition of the weather.

In his quarter century of climbing, nothing ever got this far. On Mount McKinley, a blizzard pinned his team down for four days in a snow cave. Four days! And they had gone on to the 20,230 foot summit and descended without further incident. But he was well enough that whole time and with other strong partners.

Now, unlike anything Kelly had ever experienced before, came a feeling of being truly helpless on a mountain. He was stuck inside this snow cave for a reason he never fathomed would trap him. Exhaustion, profound exhaustion, compounded by dehydration and hypothermia, with hands and feet damaged by the bitter cold of that epic on the summit night - just two nights ago. But he had gone four days in a snow cave on McKinley!

At age 48, Kelly is both the oldest and the most experienced of the three climbers. On the day of the summit climb he had probably led much of the hardest climbing in the 50° - 60° ice chutes, and by the time he stood on the summit area he had at least gained 5,403 vertical feet in one day. His total elevation gain had been from nearly sea level to 11,240 feet in just 48 hours. Now the effects of this also weighed down on Kelly.

Acute mountain sickness was kicking in with headache, dizziness and nausea. Outward symptoms may have included confusion, drowsiness, shortness of breath and a general feeling of general malaise.

The effort had been titanic but not without terrible cost. As an experienced climber, Kelly knew that he reached this low physical point and that if he continued he will not make the descent. It's likely Kelly also weighs into the equation a factor for his handicapping the other two men on their descent. If they make it down okay, Kelly knew they would at least be safe and initiate his rescue.

Hours slipped by. Kelly can't get warm. The internal furnace was just not firing up. The remaining food consists of half an orange. He has no working stove with fuel to burn. He has given virtually all of his equipment to his two companions. His pack is empty.

Outside the snow cave each hour brings louder and louder winds. Now it is raging like an infinitely long freight train outside his entrance. The cold is seeping in. A cave which suited three persons the first night is harder to keep warm with only one.

By the early afternoon Kelly is hoping his companions might have made it down to the car and be on their way to get rescue. Just as importantly they would be down and safe. What a relief that would be. He, Kelly, would have been partially responsible for that, as he would have insisted they go without him, that was their best shot. Maybe they got lucky.

Unfortunately, the combined years of experience between Brian and Jerry are still less than half of Kelly's 25 years. It should be Kelly leading this highly technical descent. And he would have, if he knew he could do it successfully. But he was wise enough to know that in his present state he would hold the others back. Leading a difficult descent was physically impossible for him now. He required rescue. And there was nothing more he could do.

Or was there? Everything is becoming a bit cloudy. Did he have his cell phone, that ubiquity of modern life, here with him in this absurd snow hole? There is a remote chance that he could get a signal, if the battery was still working. Maybe, just maybe there is something he can do, and that is an attempt to call home.

Home. The very word lowers blood-pressure and brightens eyes. There is no better place on Earth than home, no place more defining of our existence than our homes. This snow cave was no home. It was a tomb. Kelly knew that.

If his friends got down the mountain, and rescue was truly

coming his way, then this call home would be for reassurance. But if not, it was going to have to be a good-bye to those he loved most. As a climber Kelly knew the difference and he would have to cover both.

He pulled out the cell phone kept warm in his pocket. It was the one he kept on him at all times in his normal life back in Dallas. It was so casual then, just another little modern tool. But here on the side of Mount Hood, Kelly could not help marvel in both fear and hope about whether this small cell phone was going to be able to work when he most desperately needed it to.

The moment of turning on the phone burns with the most profound anxiety. At the sound of successful powering-up of the cell phone comes a pang of hope. Pressing the tiny buttons is impossible in gloves, and so he removes one in order to press the buttons and make his call. Of course, he has a speed dial to home.

The button is pressed, and a call initiates at 3:45pm on Sunday December 10th. As the signal roams the stormy Cascades in search of a connecting tower, those few seconds grow to an eternity. Then the familiar sounds of the phone connecting to his home. Finally, over that tiny pinnacle of modern technology, come the familiar voices of his beloved family; first his two children and then his wife, Karen. Then Kelly James began his last four minute call home from the heights of Mount Hood.

The incident took place in Hood River County, Oregon, and fell under the jurisdiction of Sheriff Joe Wampler. A steadying presence and excellent spokesman, Sheriff Wampler was involved from the very outset of the rescue effort. (Photo Credit: 939th Air Refueling Wing/Dept. of Defense)

Search and Rescue Efforts
(December 10th -20th, 2006)

On that first Sunday, December 10th, the cell phone call from Kelly James to his wife Karen and family alerts authorities to the situation on the mountain. This happens in real-time, as recalled by Hood River County Sheriff Joe Wampler, exclusively to KGW TV in Portland:

> "Karen James called and says, 'I've got Kelly on the phone.' That just changed the complexity of the world. I've got a live guy, at the summit of Mount Hood, talking to his wife on the phone - alive. Her son's talking to Kelly on the phone. She is talking to me on the phone. Ask him where he's at - you know - we get that conversation going. Are you okay? Ya, he says he's okay. He's wet, he's cold. But I know Kelly, something's wrong. I mean, he doesn't sound good to me. Stay right where you're at. Save the battery on your phone. Call in every once in a while. Do not leave your phone on. And they were repeating what I was saying right to him. Okay and then, a, oh a heart-jerker happened then. I could hear her yelling at him to 'Stay awake. Us and the kids have just put the tree up and it'll be here when you get home.'"

This immediately kicks the machinery of the Search and Rescue into high gear. From the sheriff's first-hand knowledge of a confirmed mountain climbing accident in progress began the domino effect of agencies contacting agencies, and climbing rescue teams being notified of the situation and told to prepare for the difficult search in the days ahead.

Searchers have only a stark set of accepted facts. First, there is one climber stuck in a snow cave, possibly injured, somewhere high on the mountain. From the cell phone conversation, it's learned that his two climbing partners had left the snow cave on

Saturday, the day before the call. And that the two men were definitely going for rescue. The mystery remained - why had Kelly stayed behind in the snow cave? His family felt there could have been no other reason than an injury. But Kelly never mentioned a specific injury during the call.

What follows is a day by day summary of the search and rescue activities and the findings of these efforts.

Sunday, December 10th, Climber's Day 4, with the cell phone call logged at 3:45pm Pacific Time, there is scarcely any daylight available for anyone to head out onto the slopes of Mount Hood. In near-by Portland, official sunset occurred at 4:27pm. Nonetheless, the sheriffs in the counties surrounding Mount Hood are notified. Also notified are Search and Rescue organizations across the region, the Federal government and a literal cascade of fellow human beings willing to search for these three missing climbers.

Monday, December 11th, Climber's Day 5, rangers from the Hood River National Forest office reveal that the first clue found on the ground is a note written by the three climbers and dropped off at the ranger station on their way up to the North Face, last Thursday, December 7th. It had been stuck in a near-by wood bin before any staff was at the station, it must have been before 7:30am, the usual starting time for most folks in the office. The climbers say they will attempt the couloirs on the North Face, to the right of Eliot Glacier, with minimal gear, and bivouac sacks for sleeping in. They also say they have experience, and left their names. Their trail has been picked up.

Now two and two are coming together. The wife of climber Kelly James, Karen, has already begun the call-out to authorities late the day before. Now, the identities of the climbers and the details of the party are solidified. In the first news stories of the day, the names of the climbers are not yet made public, but by early afternoon the name of Kelly James is acknowledged. He is the man stuck in the snow cave.

Hood River County Sheriff Joe Wampler takes over-all responsibility for the Search and Rescue operation. Search and Rescue teams are converging on Mount Hood from Hood River, Portland, and many other cities in the region.

Among the many heroic forces that are setting about searching for these climbers are the members of the leading edge of the ground search, the so-called "hasty teams." These are the expert teams who go first and fastest to the most likely places on a mountain where the missing might have ended up. Essentially, they scour the most probable areas first, allowing them to narrow the search focus, by ruling out where they have searched.

Searchers in a blizzard at 11:15AM on the first Monday, December 11th, 2006. Typical weather encountered by the searchers during the frustrating first week of search and rescue for the three climbers on Mount Hood. (Photo Credit: Todd Wells/304th Search and Rescue Squadron)

Two search and rescue hasty teams take to the slopes of Mount Hood, on the south and north sides, in hopes of finding the two descending climbers. Ideally, the teams will meet up at the summit, and look for the stranded climber Kelly James in a snow cave. The northside team alone consists of 18 seasoned search and rescue climbers. But as the afternoon wears on, the weather gets worse. Above tree line it is virtually a white-out. No helicopters are able to take off today, and so the day ends with frustration but still hope for the three.

Tuesday, December 12th, Climber's Day 6, the sense of urgency permeates the growing search effort. Incredibly, at 1am the Corvallis Search and Rescue sends a team of five people up the mountain from their established camp of the north side of Mount Hood. At 6am three Hood River Crag Rats leave to search the higher slopes. By 9 am another four teams of five people from the Portland Mountain Rescue and Pacific Northwest Search and Rescue all begin combing the slopes above the northside camp.

Communications are being coordinated by members of Mountain Wave, a volunteer group that provides short-wave radio communications in emergency situations. At lower elevation it is calm with light snow. The strategy is to send the teams on different potential descent routes off the North Face and Cooper Spur. If Brian and Jerry have made it off the higher slopes they might be found along these typical descent paths. During this small window of opportunity, the ground troops are giving their all to find the two climbers if they have made it this far.

Meanwhile, the technical folks are working on triangulating where on the mountain the cell phone call two days prior came from. It involves digging through databases of cell phone calls, finding the coordinates of cell towers which relayed the signal and making some calculations as to where the originating signal may have come from. They generally portray this position as being on the North Face at approximately 11,000 feet above sea level, but there is no certain way to know exactly where, high on Mount Hood the signal, the snow cave and Kelly James are truly located.

Wednesday, December 13ᵗʰ, Climber's Day 7, brings the over-all worst weather to the Pacific Northwest of this entire month of December. Cold winds and icy rain at the base of Mount Hood keep searchers from going much beyond tree line. "Mother Nature is holding us back," says Bernie Wells, the search coordinator for the locally based Crag Rats Mountain Rescue Team.

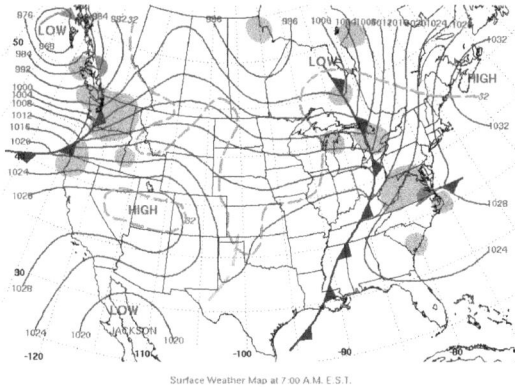

Surface Weather Map at 7:00 A.M. E.S.T.

A surface weather map for December 13ᵗʰ 2006 shows the most powerful storm which hit during December. This is one weather obstacle preventing rescuers from getting to the scene sooner. Many people mistakenly link this storm to the start of the climb - it actually delayes searchers but does not affect the climbers. (Source: NOAA archives)

The search is focused on the lower slopes and canyons where Brian and Jerry could end up. Surely, if their bid for the base is successful, they will be near treeline and dig themselves a snow cave. After such an effort, they will need rest and protection from the elements - although their situation should be less dire than Kelly's. Searchers can not go above the 7000 foot level due to high winds, clocking 60mph at Base Camp. Even with the difficult weather, everything that can be tried is. Including the use of an unmanned, heat-seeking drone aircraft, launched in the afternoon, but it detects nothing and has to come down after only a short while due to high winds. By the end of the day the Northwest Weather and Avalanche Center issues a "High" avalanche warning, especially in the 7,000 foot level and below but also at the higher elevations. In these conditions the triggering of avalanches is likely even with small additional loads. According to Capt. Chris Bernard of the U.S. Air Force 304th Rescue Squadron, "The search area is the whole mountain."

Thursday, December 14th , Climber's Day 8, brings the highest winds to Mount Hood for the entire month of December. While conditions the days before had been extreme in wind and low visibility, this punch from the storm brings precipitation in addition to even higher winds. At 11,000 feet wind gusts are estimated to be 130mph. Power is knocked out in the region to one million homes and businesses. It is absolutely impossible for rescuers to be on Mount Hood. A final tally due to the storm is at least ten, perhaps as many as fourteen people in the region dying in storm-related events. This is as extreme as weather ever gets on Mount Hood.

Friday, December 15th, Climber's Day 9, before dawn the weather system looks like it will break. Forecast calls for dry and clear. Ambitious plans are set afoot; a team of 30 readies to search the North Face while another 40 prepares on the south side. They leave at first light. The mountain over 8,000 feet is being put off limits to other adventure-seeking climbers. Hopes are high that two Black Hawk helicopters from the Oregon Army National Guard will be able to fly to the summit with medics. A third helicopter will join the search in the air. If any of the climbers are found, they will be flown to a Portland hospital. As the afternoon wears on the weather deteriorates, the winds pick up and all searchers get called back off the mountain.

Saturday, December 16th, Climber's Day 10, in the early morning the winds have calmed down to where the full compliment of searchers deploys in hopes of finding the three climbers. There is a plan to build a high camp for rescuers at 9,000 feet on the south side. The hasty team immediately sets out for the summit. Helicopters take flight and comb the mountainsides for any sign of the missing climbers. All the stops are being pulled out and a complete search quickly gathers steam, attempting to converge and gain control of a summit foothold. They will search that area, and then the North Face. At mid-morning a rumor flies that two climbers have been spotted by helicopter, and resources are diverted and focused on a possible air rescue - but by noon this is given up as having been a false report. Afternoon winds grow stronger, gusting to 50mph. The hasty team struggles up to the 10,000 foot level until the winds make further progress impossible. But this is the highest point any search team has gotten yet. With the weather again turning unfavorable the teams have to pull back. Attempts to build a high camp are snafued. But the search continues using technology to possibly locate the climbers. Two C-130 airplanes fitted with thermal imaging equipment will be flying the mountain through the night. Any living human in plain sight would light up their screen like a Christmas tree light, but a man snug inside a snow cave would be virtually invisible. The afternoon light is fading, it is a day of disappointment for the ground searchers. Then, with the last little bit of sunset still visible a Black Hawk helicopter flying high against the North Face spots "anomalies in the snow" and unidentified items, possibly some climbing equipment, several hundred feet down the North Face from the summit. If it proves to be equipment from the climbers, then it suggests where they might be or have been. It is the best potential piece of physical evidence found on the mountain. There is a renewed hope, a clue has been discovered. But it is too late to do anything more until first light. Throughout the night hope burns strongly that all three men might still be alive. Searchers prepare to flood the mountain early the next day.

On the last flight of the day, December 16th, the Black Hawk helicopter spots evidence of the climbers high on the North Face of Mount Hood. (Photo Credit: Faith Cathcart/The Oregonian)

Sunday, December 17th, Climber's Day 11, is finally a beautiful, clear, windless day on Mount Hood. Well before dawn the hasty team takes snow cats to 9,200 feet and heads up the south side. Not long after first light, helicopters launch to reconnaissance the specific spot on the North Face where something was spotted the night before and they confirm the presence of climbing gear high on the North Face.

At noon a Chinook helicopter with six members of the 304th Rescue Squadron of the U.S. Air Force Reserve takes off for the summit. This elite team is made up of what the military calls pararescuemen, the most highly trained in every rescue situation imaginable, and two medics who are trained to blunt the traumas encountered in war and peace. Pilots, seasoned in Afghanistan and Iraq, are going to try to drop the team as close to a position directly over the site as possible. With them are four rescuers from the Portland Mountain Rescue and the Hood River Crag Rats.

The searchers coming from the south side reach the summit and quickly traverse over to join the air lifted team. They set up a descent down to the site with climbing gear visible. Down these ropes come the most elite of the rescuers, cameras rolling show a dozen people above the point. Rescuers descend to the site, approximately 300 feet below the summit.

About 1pm they arrive at what the media reports as a "snow cave" with one sleeping pad, some rope and two ice axes in it. The public will know this as the first "snow cave" but after careful investigation the more correct designation is a "snow platform." This clarification never appears in the media. It is a platform because it is a relatively shallow cut in the side of the mountain. The platform is deep enough to provide some temporary protection from the wind but not deep enough to spend a night in. Searchers even dig deeper into the side of the mountain to make sure no one is buried there.

The snow platform is a stop for the climbers on ascent but not built deep enough for an overnight. A. Searcher investigates on December 17th (Photo Credit: Todd Wells/304th Search and Rescue Squadron)

They note that the platform is more substantial than the typical one made by climbers who are passing through as fast as possible. This snow platform is embellished to provide some wind break, enough for three men to stop and gather themselves and plan the next moves. It is not substantial enough to spend a night inside of and survive.

There is understandable confusion among everyone concerning when this location was used by the climbers. The searchers actually dig until they hit rock because in the week that has passed a tremendous amount of new snow has fallen and wind has blown everything to a fuzzy semblance of what it was like the week before. It quickly becomes apparent there are no climbers there but when did they use this place? For the moment it will remain a mystery.

On the floor of this snow platform searchers find a piece of insulated padding. On top of this is part of a climbing rope. Approximately 60 feet of this rope had been cut out of the middle and is missing. The remaining rope pieces have been doubled with a single overhand knot in the middle. The cuts are clean, intentional. The tied, doubled, roped is just sitting on the floor of the platform, attached to nothing.

Also on the floor of the snow platform are two ice tools described as 18-inch Blue Ice Petzels. Each climber presumably has two ice tools. The typical combination is an ice axe - usually over 20 inches in length and an ice hammer, say 15 inches to 20 inches in length. This makes a total of six ice climbing tools between the three climbers. When climbing the steepest part of the North Face both tools have to be used. Leaving behind tools is a very serious action, intentional or unintentional. It appears these were intentionally left behind.

Immediately outside the snow platform is the "Y" shape of a climbing anchor, fixed to the side of the mountain. The anchor points are aluminum snow pickets, spears of aluminum than can be sunk into a snow face, from which sling webbing is connected and used to anchor the climbers while they spend time at the snow platform. The presence of a rock in the photograph distinguished the snow platform from the finding later in the day.

48

A Press Release by the Department of Defense that is widely viewed in the media shows the "Y" anchor in the snow at the platform. (Photo Credit: 939th Air Refueling Wing/Dept. of Defense, HO)

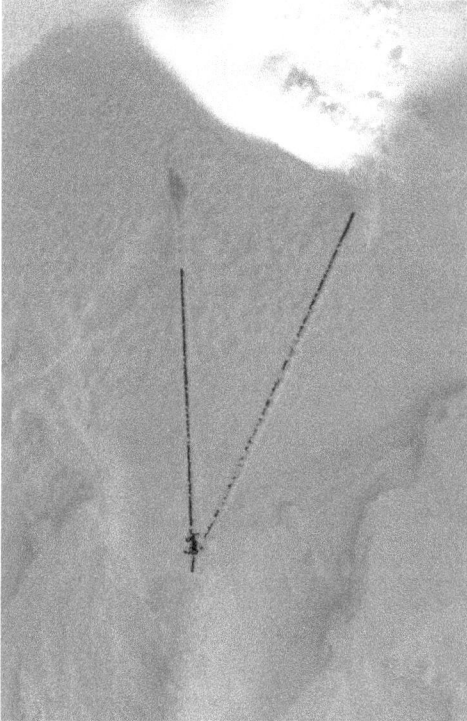

On the day of the discovery the media mistakenly promotes the idea that this "Y" is an intentional signal from the climbers. Only a few level-headed climbers interviewed on television express doubt about this interpretation. The media amplifies this unlikely idea until actual rescuers get to the site and identified it as a climbing anchor. Yet, the fact that this equipment remains at the site suggests they think it would not be needed later. Same with the ice tools, and the stands of rope left behind. This all suggests that the climbers are not thinking of returning to such steep ground again on Mount Hood.

From the snow platform, searchers identify tracks from the climbers frozen into the snowfield leading up to the summit area of Mount Hood. The tracks are faint and in the photograph below the tracks cannot be resolved. It has been over one week since they were made, but enough are still visible to be tracked by the expert searchers on the scene. In the final analysis they determine that three sets of tracks run parallel up to the summit from the snow platform.

A Press Release by the Department of Defense shows footprints frozen in the snow. Three sets of tracks run parallel up the summit snowfield from the snow platform. Taken on December 18th, 2006. (Photo Credit: 939th Air Refueling Wing/Dept. of Defense, HO)

The rescuers who are lower to the scene also search the nearby area for evidence. In ever increasing circles they investigate the surrounding area. In mid afternoon, while scouting the surrounding area, the team discovers a true snow cave. This snow cave is large enough to provide shelter for a night's survival.

At 3:45pm they enter this snow cave and find the body of a climber - exactly, to the minute, seven days after Kelly James made his cell phone call to home. But it is too late in the day to be able to bring down the body. They look carefully for any identifying information. They find a non-working, water-logged cell phone in the climbers' pocket.

News is quickly radioed down to the coordination center, the code word used is at first leaving many confused, then it comes through that "a climber's dead body has been found." Yet, even at the end of this day, there is official hope for the other two climbers.

However, it had been the second good, clear day on the mountain. If Brian and Jerry were still alive, even the most inexperienced of armchair mountaineer is saying to himself, if they are alive they would have surfaced by now.

Monday, December 18th, Climber's Day 12, with the news of a deceased climber found late the day before in a snow cave at the 11,000 foot level on Mount Hood, came a cold dose of unpleasant reality. It set the main task for today as being the recovery of the body from the snow cave on the dangerous high slopes.

A Chinook helicopter with pararescuers and members of the local Crag Rats are tasked with this retrieval. In the morning, Jessica Nunez, acting as a spokeswoman for the family, broke the news to the public that the body of the deceased climber is, indeed, that of climber Kelly James.

Today things have turned decidedly negative in the Search and Rescue. Two Black Hawk helicopters are going to fly in search of Brian and Jerry. Ground search crews are going to comb the lower levels on the north side in case the climbers got that far down and are holed up in a snow cave.

Members of the search and rescue team at the entrance to the snow cave where Kelly James was found, December 18th. (Photo Credit: Todd Wells/304th Search and Rescue Squadron)

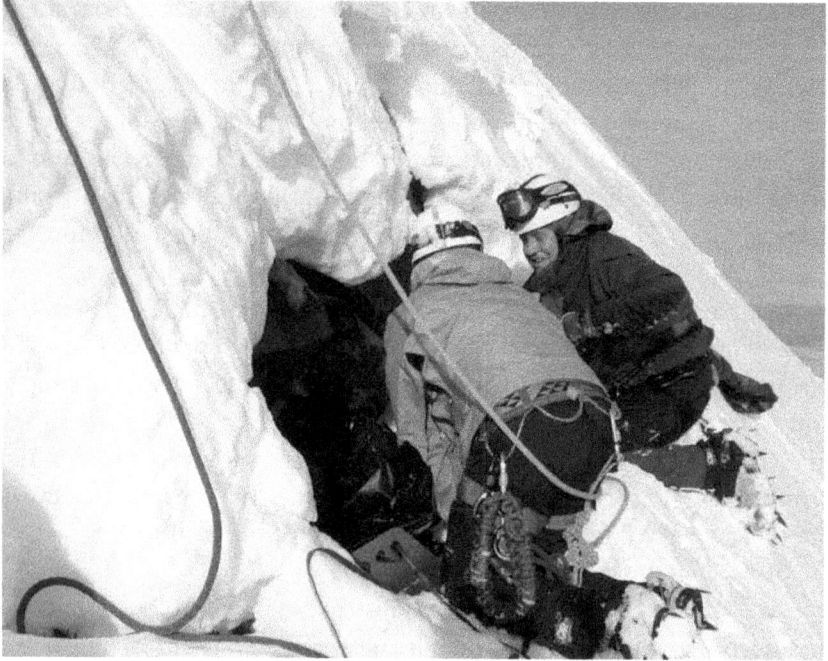

Hood River Sheriff Joe Wampler, in a morning news conference, outlines a theory of what happened to the two other climbers. He explains that the two men left Kelly James in his snow cave and were trying to descend to get help. From what was found at the scene of the unoccupied "snow cave" included two ice axes and some rope. Knowing how crucial the ice axes would be to life on a 60° angle ice slope made the sheriff very concerned. He went on to say that the two had probably fallen from that position.

By the end of the day the ground crews find no one. The Black Hawks see nothing. The Chinook removes the body of Kelly James, and hopes have been cruelly shattered. Weather forecasts another storm moving into the area by Wednesday. The last window for searching is coming to a close.

Tuesday, December 19th, Climbers Day 13, the camera recovered with Kelly James has photos which chronicle the men's climb on Mount Hood. It is reported by the sheriff that the three men appear leaving the car as smiling, confident friends at the start of a great adventure. Later pictures show them on the Eliot Glacier.

The last photo is a classic shot of ice climbing on the steep ice of Mount Hood's North Face. (Above 10,000 feet.) Everything appears to be going smoothly. Although these photos are never released to the public, they give the sheriff, rescuers, and the family some general benchmarks in time. This is what is worrisome about that last photograph - the intensity of daylight, the angle of the sun, shadows suggest later afternoon and the men are still climbing up the North Face. There is no photo on the top of Mount Hood at 11,239 feet elevation.

Wednesday, December 20th, Climbers Day 14, is the day that officials acknowledge that the search and rescue for climbers Brian Hall and Jerry Cooke is over and that it is now a search and recovery effort. All hope vanishes. Results of the autopsy on Kelly James are reported. There was no disabling injuries, he died of hypothermia complicated by dehydration. Time of death was estimated to have been not long after his phone call on December 10th. Probably not later than the next day.

Regardless of the precise time, the painful absence of two returning, live, climbers ten days later is acknowledged on Wednesday December 20th when the official search and rescue effort is ended. Weather is again moving into the region, and the mountain again becomes unapproachable. More snow falls. It becomes too dangerous to send a search and recovery team. As of that day it became a recovery effort for victims Brian and Jerry.

February, 2007, Members of the 304th Search and Rescue Squadron search the upper Eliot Glacier and base of the North Face from the ground but find nothing.

July, 2007, Searchers find the climber's cache of gear next to the Tilly Jane hut, under a board. In includes a significant number of items useful for survival.

The media attention brought to this American climbing accident is huge and perhaps unprecedented. Millions watch live coverage of the search via satellite transmission from media vans like these in the Mount Hood area during December 2006. (Photo Credit: 939th Air Refueling Wing/Dept. of Defense)

The Media
(December 11th -20th, 2006)

The media smelled a potential Christmas miracle in the story of the stranded climbers which surfaced late on Sunday, December 10th with a confirmed call from a stranded climber, Kelly James, high on Mount Hood, to his family in Dallas Texas. As details appeared, the story-line, the characters, and the potential for the good guys to pull one out was increasingly appealing to media and viewers alike. There were two weeks for the climbers to be found alive as of December 11th, 2006, and it was fed to the public in as positive a spin as possible.

The first play schedule reference to the Mount Hood situation on CNN was on its Newsroom show on Monday, December 11th. It was listed as the twentieth item in a 29 item play list. A modest blip for a story that, over the next ten days was going to rocket to the top of national cable and network news programs.

In this, one of the earliest, if not the earliest, news stories, CNN cut to affiliate KPTV, out of Portland Oregon. The reporter, Mark Glyzewski, is live at the base of Mount Hood in late morning, speaking to anchor Kyra Phillips. Mark refers to these men as "hikers" and also as "climbers." Here, I believe, is the origin of the inconsistency which confused viewers for days to come - the "hiker" versus "climber" designation of our three climbers. Mark of KPTV explained,

> "And searchers have been at it for about five and a half hours today so far. Still no sign of these three missing hikers. There's actually a two-pronged effort going on right now. There's a group of about 18 searchers making their way up the north side of Mt. Hood. Again, this is an 11,000-foot peak... Also, there's another group coming up from Timberline Lodge from the south. They're hoping to intersect at some point, hopefully today, but it is very slow going. You can see the weather conditions here just

miserable. They have rain here at 4,000-foot level. We're told just minutes ago that at least one of the groups have made it up to about the 6,500-foot level. As for the climbers, again, these three have not been seen or heard from since yesterday afternoon."

Clearly, no hikers at the 11,000 elevation of Mount Hood in early winter - only climbers, bold, risk-taking climbers. For days some networks would run the Mount Hood stories headlining them as "hikers" one hour and then as "climbers" in the next segment. Nonetheless, this was the beginning salvo of a climbing story which ran farther and higher than just about any climbing story ever. Certainly it will be a landmark in climbing history as one of the first incidents to be covered in the national, real-time media of the twenty-first century.

A brief study of just one popular cable show the CNN Anderson Cooper 360 indicates just how this story took root and became a dominant media event of the month and then dropped off the radar. In the first two nights of the Mount Hood story breaking, Anderson Cooper 360 already had programmed extensive time of the wrap-up of the James Kim Family Ordeal (father tried to hike out and died, wife and two children survived in the stuck car and were rescued days later) in another Oregon Mountain range which aired on December 10th and 11th.

The news segue between outdoor sagas December 10-12, 2006, in the American media.

Oregon		Mount Hood
James Kim		3 Climbers
Family Ordeal	===>	Stranded
And Tragedy		1 in snow cave
1 Fatality		2 gone for rescue
3 Survive		Oregon

On December 12th the Mount Hood story first hit the Anderson Cooper 360 show as the first item on the bottom half hour of the one hour show. The next day it rose into the first half hour of the show and again was mentioned in the second half of the show. On December 14th, 15th the Mount Hood story was the lead story. All of this was based on the live, person-to-person cell phone call of the previous Sunday, December 10th between Kelly James and his family and the cascade of discoveries and rumors since.

Over the course of seven consecutive shows, almost 14% of all the headlines and stories on Anderson Cooper 360 were about the Mount Hood Search and Rescue. On a peak day it was one of four stories extensively covered.

For eight days and nights the coverage of the stranded climbers on Mount Hood was all about hope, with a capital "H." Every possible hope for the climbers was explored. No one dared pronounce them gone. And the media was able to find a few hopeful examples, even on Climber's Day 9, December 15th, 2006.

There surfaced a remarkable story of three teenagers who survived 13 nights pinned down in a snow cave on Mount Hood. It was New Year's Eve 1975 when three young men, Randy Knapp (then 18), Gary Schneider (16) and Matt Meacham (16) set out from Timberline Lodge to climb the south side. They were well-prepared, with ten days of food, a stove and fuel, sleeping bags, down coats, a tent and climbing gear. One of the boys' father taught mountaineering at a near-by college. Two of the boys had climbed Mount Hood before, and made other major summits in the region. It was Matt's first mountain climb.

It took two days slogging up the mountains to position themselves for a summit attempt. But conditions forced them back to a snow cave their third day out, compounded by heavy snow and whiteout conditions. Agreeing to descend, they get lost. Schneider and Knapp fall into crevasses but self-rescued. Realizing they are off-route, they over-correct, like many others have done, towards Zigzag Canyon. After spending one miserable night in a platform tent at 7,600 feet, in 40mph winds, and they unanimously agreed to use snow caves from then on. The next day they climbed to near Illumination Rock and dig a snow cave, which they are pinned down in for the next 13 nights by a horrendous storm. Ten days into the misadventure they hear a helicopter searching for them but cannot make contact. The same day they run out of food.

The snow cave is incredibly successful. Almost too successful, it keeps temperatures just above freezing and melt gets everything wet, keeping them colder than they would have been in bitter cold which kept inside temperatures just below freezing. They really did not have water-proof gear, but they manage. Even using the melt for drinking water, keeping them from becoming fatally dehydrated. They have a bible and read extensively from it, proving faith is an ingredient of survival.

Seventeen days from the expectant New Year's Eve departure, the boys, really men by now, dig themselves out of their snow cave for the last time. Incredibly, there is another 15 feet of snow on top of their original snow cave. The tunnel entrance, which had been continuously cleaned to allow fresh air circulation and escape, was now 40 feet long! Seeing clear skies that morning they made a break and met up with rescuers, including Schneider's father on the slopes. The boys suffered no more injury than minor frostbite on toes and fingers. But as for celebritizing the story - no. The narrator, Randy Knapp, has been silent over these years but on this day, the Climber's 9th Day, the media shares his story of hope in a headline, "Survivor of '76: If we made it, they can too."

Facts had barely budged since the search began five days prior. Weather had essentially kept the searchers at bay all this time. Through the 15th the hasty teams had not made it up to 10,000 feet, and Kelly James was probably near the 11,000 foot level. The following day of coverage was lighter but on the Sunday, one week after the cell phone call from the snow cave, the story came alive on national television.

Sunday, December 17th, was the apex of media coverage, CNN carried it live much of the afternoon until sunset in the Pacific Northwest. It was the most dramatic day of the entire search. It was when they located and focused on a "snow cave." It turned out to be not a "snow cave" but a "snow platform," However, it was always referred to as being a snow cave, to the end of the coverage in the media. This turns out to be a misnomer which confused the chain of events as first reported.

Early in the day Media focused on the sighting of some climbing gear, just outside the "snow cave". From distant telephoto shots it looked like the letter "Y". The Media quickly jumped on this as having been an intentional sign left by the climbers, to alert the world to their location.

For hours the Media ridiculously pondered on this idea of a message from the climbers. Once real search and rescue climbers got on the scene they quickly identified this as a belay anchor. Late in the afternoon, breaking news came of the discovery of another snow cave. Quickly following that news flash came word that a body had been discovered in the newly found snow cave. Viewers were left not knowing which climber had been discovered. The press said it was waiting for confirmation and for the families to be notified. When the news cycle ended that day audiences were left with the cliff-hanger of who was the victim on that lonely mountain.

Most hopes were dashed with this discovery, although searchers did not want to rule out the slim possibility that Brian and Jerry were somehow low on the mountain, tucked into a snow cave, surviving - perhaps buried by new snows that make it difficult for them to get out. That they were so exhausted that they could not budge from the snow cave.

Sadly, in a rapid turn of event, the last best hope for a complete Christmas miracle was crushed.

My own viewer notes for the CBS Nightly News with Katie Couric pick up on Monday, December18th where the lead story was the grim news from Mount Hood that a body found the day before in a snow cave was the body of climber Kelly James. Same lead for the NBC Nightly News with Brian Williams.

Also, on the 19th, the Mount Hood story was the lead story for CBS. On the day the search was called off, December 20th, Mount Hood was the second story.

The machinery of television big ratings kicked in.

The follow-up on Thursday the 21st was the face-to-face interview with Karen James. It was conducted in Karen James own home, with a gas lite fire place in the background. This was just four days after the grizzly discovery. Yet, Karen James remained cerebral, stoic, and comforted by her religion. It was the kind of brave face a wife puts on if she believes in the fight her man went through.

The Mount Hood story reached a natural stopping point. A tragedy with one climber dead and recovered, and two climbers missing and presumed dead. There was little for headline news remaining for now. There was no Christmas miracle on Mount Hood.

What had taken up an enormous amount of media attention for almost two weeks was over. Any deeper understanding, clarifications, mis-statements which ought to be clarified, have not been offered so far. Besides the kick-start of confusion about "hikers" versus "climbers" mentioned earlier, and the discussion of the "Y"-signal from the climbers, at least two others deserve clarification.

Beginning on Sunday, December 17th, the public learned of two snow caves being found. Inside one was the deceased climber Kelly James. In the real-time of television coverage of this event, it was actually the real snow cave that was discovered near the very end of this day, . Most of the coverage on the 17th was about the "snow cave" with the "Y" of rope. The description as a "snow cave" was never deviated in the coverage. However, it turns out, the "snow cave" was actually a well-built "snow platform" as discussed in the Analysis Chapter.

But the climbing interest vacuum was quickly filled by another breaking story of missing American climbers in China. Although they had last been seen in November the media was now reporting, at first without names, details forthcoming in the next few days.

Final American news segue between outdoor sagas December 2006.

Oregon	Oregon	China
James Kim	Mount Hood	2 Climbers
Family Ordeal ==>	3 Climbers Have ==>	Missing Since
And Tragedy	Winter Epic	November
1 Recovered	1 Recovered	1 Recovered
3 Survive	2 presumed deceased	1 Missing
Search & Rescue	Rescue Halted	Search/Recovery
Completed	Recovery in Summer	On-going

Stunning Discoveries of August 2007 About Media Myths

A research trip to the Mount Hood area in August 2007 revealed what could be learned after the dust settled from the original frenetic coverage of the incident. Upon meeting one of the actual searchers who found the snow cave with Kelly, it was revealed that the snow cave with Kelly James inside was actually on the East Face of Mount Hood, not the North Face!

From virtually the outset of this accident, media maps and diagrams showed Kelly James possible location as being on the North Face, just below the very summit of Mount Hood. It became emblazoned in America's collective mind that these brave souls had reached the summit and descended back down the North Face.

The North Face location of the snow cave is clearly the single greatest myth propagated by the media that was never properly cleared up - until this book. Indeed, the snow platform discussed earlier was on the North Face, as part of the climber's ascent route. But the omni-present snow cave said with such certainty by the media to be on the North Face was actually on the East Face.

A Brief History of Mount Hood Accidents

The number of climbers who attempt Mount Hood in recent years has grown to an estimated 10,000 per year. One source of climbing accident reports are the **Accidents In North American Mountaineering** volumes which began in 1947. The American Alpine Club (AAC) compiles reports from collaborating groups and individuals across North America. Only select cases are written up and published in the annual report. There may be other cases from the same state which are tallied but no narrative is provided. The location descriptions of the accidents allows all the Mount Hood cases to be brought together and briefly analyzed here.

As in any volunteer endeavor, there were years when no data was incoming from certain states. Thus, in some (probably most) years when zero accidents were found reported from Mount Hood it may be an artifact of having no reports either submitted, incomplete reporting of all accidents which actually occurred, or not having the narrated which reveals the detailed location of Mount Hood.

In a review of sixty years of Accidents In North American Mountaineering volumes a total of 53 climbing accidents on Mount Hood were narrated in the volumes. This directly involved a total of 285 climbers and multiples more persons involved in the search and rescues which followed. A total of 36 deaths were due to having a climbing accident on Mount Hood.

The most deadly Mount Hood climbing accident occurred in May, 1986. It was spring with unpredictable weather; at the border for folks with a choice to go climbing. It had snowed the two days before they started, and more snow and rain were forecast - the leader was aware of this. However, the leader of the school adventure group, a 44 year old male, wanted to keep a schedule, since they had planned a series of such climbs with no make-up time by the end of the semester. He was seasoned and had attempted the mountain 18 times, reaching the summit on six occasions, and turning back 12 other attempts.

63

They began at 2:30am on the south side, breaking deep snow. Throughout the morning some in the group turned back. They had discussed descent several times, and had several chances to back-off as a group. However, the leader was adamant about giving it "one more try." Then he and a few of the still strong disappeared ahead of the rest of the group. It was probably early afternoon when a bedraggled leader and his small crew came back down from an unsuccessful attempt, telling the others to turn back immediately.

But by this time the weather was caving in, high winds and snow reduced visibility. The group of thirteen eventually had to dig a snow cave in horrendous blizzard conditions - but had only one shovel between them to do the work! People had to rotate in and out of the snow cave all night. Important survival gear was left outside, snowed-over, and went unused. By morning several, including the leader, were suffering from severe hypothermia. Two in the team determined that they had to get rescue and headed off the next morning as the storm quieted.

In the next 48 hours nine climbers died of hypothermia before rescuers reached them. Only two teens walked out alive. Incredibly, the location of their snow cave was just a few hundred yards laterally from the top of the Palmer ski lift (elevation 8,500 feet). The American Alpine Club spear-headed investigation summarized the factors involved in this terrible outcome as: "Improper Decision - Failure to turn back, fatigue, exposure, hypothermia, inadequate equipment, weather, failure to follow route."

Every climbing accident provides lessons. Just two of the many salient features of this accident include the fact that it occurred in the vicinity of only 8,500 feet of elevation, on the less technical side of the mountain, in spring - and it only took 72 hours for nine persons to succumb to exposure and hypothermia. This becomes the largest contributor of fatalities in the climbing history of Mount Hood at nine dead. It lead to the development of the Locator Unit, a tracking device which can be triangulated during ground searches.

The following Tables present a summary of the fifty-three accidents on Mount Hood reviewed for this book. There are missing data values and small round-off errors which effect the total numbers and percentages in the tables. The purpose here is to present a reasonable sample of the most serious accidents that have happened on Mount Hood and share the accident pattern with readers.

Table 1: Summary of Mount Hood reports from Accidents in North American Mountaineering 1947-2004.

Number of accidents narrated: 53
Total number of person involved: 285
Total number of fatalities: 36
Total number of fatal Accidents: 15

Direction of Travel (Number, Percent):
Ascent   10   20%
Descent   40   80%

Routes grouped into sides of Mount Hood (approximate):

	Fatal		Non-Fatal		Total Accidents	
South	5	21%	19	79%	24	(48%)
West	2	17%	10	83%	12	(24%)
North	7	58%	5	42%	12	(24%)
East	0	0%	0	0%	0	(0%)
Summit Area	1	50%	1	50%	2	(4%)
	15		35		50	(100%)

The 53 accidents involved a total of 285 people. Thirty-six climbers died in fifteen accidents on Mount Hood. Almost half these accidents occurred on the South side. However, the most deadly side was the North side. Of the 12 accidents reported from the North side of Mount Hood, 7 involved fatalities. That means 56% of those accidents involved a fatality. Among the South side accidents 21% involved one or more fatalities.

A breakdown of accidents by direction of travel found 20% on ascent while 80% on descent. This seems to be a highly skewed result which can also be interpreted as four of five accidents happened on descent. However, there are cases were weather turned back the climber and so they were on descent when the accident occurred. It also conjures the usual notions about fatigue, underestimation of the mountain, and technical skills. Clearly a warning to future climbers to watch the descent carefully.

Table 2: Month Accidents Occurred In (Number, Percent) :					
January	3	6%	July	7	13%
February	1	2%	Aug.	4	7%
March	2	4%	Sept.	4	7%
April	3	8%	Oct.	3	6%
May	11	21%	Nov.	0	0%
June	15	28%	Dec.	0	0%

The seasonal breakdown appears to highlight May and June as high accident months, probably reflection the higher use in springtime. There were no narrative reports for the months of November or December over the 57 years of reports reviewed, which included through the year 2004. This quickly brings us to an analysis of the factors involved in these accidents.

Table 3: Factors Influencing Mount Hood Accidents.	Yes (No., %)	No (No., %)
Did they exceed their ability?	28, 54%	24, 46%
Were they roped?	23, 44%	29, 56%
Was weather a factor?	14, 27%	38, 73%
Was gear a factor in accident?	14, 27%	38, 73%
Was wind a factor?	13, 25%	39, 75%
Did they fail to follow the route?	11, 22%	40, 78%
Was a storm involved?	7, 14%	44, 86%
Was an avalanche involved?	6, 12%	46, 88%
Was darkness a factor?	6, 12%	46, 88%

In the AAC cases, exceeding ones ability was the most common single factor in the accidents. This was followed by being unroped. Weather, including wind and a storm, was a factor in just over one quarter of these cases. Issues with gear were also involved in a quarter of these cases. Route finding problems struck one fifth the cases. Avalanche and darkness were cited in only a bit more than one in ten cases. Many other factors clearly influence the survivability of the accidents including the elevation but the data is too scarce to make a clear statistical analysis.

Party size obviously influenced many dynamics on a climb. In general a rope team consists of two climbers. The next natural unit is two ropes teams of two climbers. In short, climbing teams with an even number of people make the most logistical sense. Three on a rope can become cumbersome and when technical climbing begins causes more time to be wasted. Table three illustrates the propensity of the accidents on Mount Hood to involve the odd numbered teams. The last statistics the author will serve to the reader in this chapter.

Table 4: Odd Climber out in parties of 10 of less.

Team Size # Climbers	Number of Accidents.	Team Size # Climbers	Number of Accidents
1	11	2	12
3	8	4	1
5	5	6	3
7	2	8	0
9	2	10	0
Odds	28 64%	Evens	16 36%

Expecting 50-50 results - the odds numbers teams are at greater risk.

Analysis

Climbers are ambitious. When there is a success on one mountain, moments later there are thoughts of the next challenge, the next big peak. That is how we do our climbing business. That is how we move ahead in our climbing lives. That is why we keep raising the stakes. Kelly, Brian and Jerry had ambition, there was even talk of trying Chomolungu, Mother Goddess of the Himalaya, Mount Everest.

Winter offers an annual opportunity for the really determined climber to find conditions as difficult as they can get. A short, easy summer rock climb can be turned into a nightmare of six hours on ice-covered granite. That trivial hand-crack can become imprisoned away from your grasp by a sheet of ice. Getting twenty feet up might take four hours, and all the guts you can muster for a weekend.

On the other hand, there are certain climbs which only exist or come into best form during the winter. These are seen by the keen-eyed climber as an opportunity to push oneself to the limit. Perhaps this motivated the climbing plan of Kelly, Brian and Jerry to attempt Mount Hood in December. While there will be climbers who take either side of this issue, listen to the first American on Mount Everest, Jim Whittaker, who said in an interview about the Mount Hood accident with CBS News correspondent Jerry Bowen:

> "'It can turn into an Everest when you get those high winds and snow. . . You get knocked over by the wind. Your goggles fog up. You can't even travel.' Most climbers attempt Mount Hood in May and June, when the weather is calmer. But Whittaker said he did not think it was reckless for the three men to climb Mount Hood during the winter. 'They were climbers that knew what they were doing. They were just pushing themselves to their farthest frontiers. That's when people are at their best,' he said."

The Climbing Plan was ambitious but doable. In the November 2006 Internet blog, Jerry "Nikko" Cooke shared the plan for Mount Hood, saying that they were aiming for a 24-36 hour ascent. By the time the climbers were at the base of Mount Hood the time estimate they left the rangers was 2-4 days. This was possible.

However, they underestimated the down-sides, were under-prepared for survival at the higher elevations, and catastrophically changed plans in a seemingly minor way - which, in the end, cost them the one-third to one-half day that might have let them get much lower down the mountain before being benighted and stormed in. This was the decision to stay the night at the Tilly Jane warming hut instead of pressing ahead higher onto the mountain to as close to the technical climbing as possible, and then spending the night in a snow cave.

What the plan lacked was a reality check - a warm-up or cool-down or a day or two testing the slopes of Mount Hood before making a full commitment. Spending a night at the base of the climb would have quickly told the climbers if they were ready to tackle the elements. More importantly, they could have been almost 2,000 feet higher on the mountain a day earlier than the summit bid.

From the perspective of some people, these men were cavalier in their approach to Mount Hood. The very notion of flying in on a Wednesday and starting up for the North Face the next day is presumptive at best, and, clearly, fatal at worst. This was the first of many, many contributing causes to this accident.

Experience, between the three climbers totaled over thirty years of climbing experience. This sounds like a lot. However, 25 of those thirty years were in one man's pocket - Kelly James. Indeed Kelly had climbed to the summits of some big mountains: Aconcagua, the highest in South America, and Mount McKinley in Alaska, the highest in North America. He had talked about trying Mount Everest and might have been after the seven summits.

Jerry Cooke had been climbing mountains for three years, His first route was Sulphide Glacier on Mount Shuskin, in Washington state. He then attended advanced climbing classes in new Hampshire and hired guide Art Mooney for private ice-climbing lessons. This meant Jerry was becoming good at the actual ice climbing but he was not becoming particularly technically skilled. As a lawyer who had come to climbing later in life, Jerry just didn't have the time to devote to becoming a technical guru. He was a competent climber, not a strong lead climber. Brian had been seriously climbing for about six years and was Kelly James' usual partner.

There is no substitution for knowledge of a mountain other than actually spending time on it. Skills and knowledge from other places and climbs are only partially transferrable to a new area. These skills may be necessary but are not always sufficient to succeed in a new climbing environment. So what the climbers had in experience took them to near the summit. It just could not get them back down. A lack of winter climbing experience was clearly a gap in the climber's resumes.

Underestimating Winter is very easy to do and these climbers did so from the very outset, building no winter fudge-factor into their climbing plan. Unless one has spent considerable time climbing, or shall I say attempting to climb in winter conditions, there can be no badge of authority. Little understanding. To successfully climb in winter all the stars must align. Weather can be the decisive factor.

However, the weather forecasts from the three days at the start of this adventure did not suggest the epic conditions that the climbers were going to encounter. On the Wednesday, December 6th, the climbers rendevous in Portland and in all likelihood encountered a forecast for the Oregon and the Mount Hood area.

Local channels would have used as their primary source of weather data the twice a day forecasts of the Northwest Weather and Avalanche Center, out of Seattle, Washington. Like every other day, at 2pm the "Mountain Weather Forecast For the Olympics, Washington Cascades and Mt Hood Area" was released. The weather forecast for the Mount Hood area are found in several sections of this extensive report (about 12 pages long) and is summarized here:

"Mostly fair and warm Wednesday afternoon through Thursday higher terrain and western slopes, but much cooler with considerable low clouds and fog lower elevations east slopes and near Gorge outflow with local freezing fog or flurries possible below about 4000 feet...Zero precipitation on Mount Hood last 24 hours...Thursday night winds at 25-40mph... freezing level at 10,000 foot level...Moderate avalanche danger above 6000 feet and low below early Wednesday. Danger slowly decreasing Wednesday and Thursday and becoming low below 7000 feet late Thursday, except for locally increasing danger on sun warmed slopes in the late morning and afternoons...Snowpack Analysis, the upper part of the snowpack primarily consists of either a thin and breakable surface crust at lower elevations and on previously sun exposed terrain or relatively shallow amounts of recent snow over a crust from Monday, mainly above 5 to 6,000 feet on sun sheltered areas. With gradual strengthening of any shallow wind slabs on north through east exposures from late last week, this snowpack is producing either a low or moderate danger."

In reading this forecast the immediate temperature and precipitation conditions appear good for Mount Hood. Avalanche danger is low. Only in the "Extended Forecast For Friday Through Sunday" can a ripple in the plan be detected.

"Gradually increasing clouds spreading northward early-mid Friday. Light rain or snow spreading slowly northward mid-late Friday with chance local freezing rain west approaches to the passes and near Columbia Gorge outflow. Light showers north, light rain or snow central and moderate rain or snow south early Saturday, with light to moderate rain or snow spreading to most areas mid-day. Light showers

Saturday afternoon, but increasing light to moderate rain or snow redeveloping Saturday night and early Sunday. Light rain or snow north and moderate rain or snow south mid-late Sunday, decreasing briefly Sunday night. Increasing rain or snow Early Monday... Snow levels 7-9000 feet early Friday, 4-6000 feet late Friday, 3-5000 feet early and late Saturday, 3-5000 feet early Sunday, 2-4000 feet late Sunday."

Reviewing these forecasts does suggest weather moving in - from the southwest. Yet, the most common adjective is "light" for rain or snow. Many readers may recall the horrific front that later slammed into the entire Pacific Northwest region area from the northwest over the following Wednesday, Thursday and Friday. That is not what hit the climbers. It turns out the forecast the climbers might have seen on Wednesday or even early Thursday morning was anything but threatening.

In contrast to these forecasts the weather tables in the back of this book estimate the conditions these climbers actually encountered on their Mount Hood climb and are based on actual data from Mount Hood Meadows Ski Area stations at 5,250 feet and 6,600 feet elevation. The Meadows Ski Area is on the Southeast side of the mountain - a fair proxy for the North Face.

The author used three parameters to make these estimates. First, the guestimated location of the climbers on Mount Hood. Second, for every 1,000 feet of elevation gain a temperature decrease of 3.7° F and, third, add 30mph to the winds clocked at 6,600 feet. Weather experts will probably latch onto the wind conversion factor and the author concedes it might be a tad too much, then add just 20mph to the winds. Nonetheless, using the adjustments suggested below the author then calculated the wind chill factor. Much has already said about these conditions high on Mount Hood that first weekend, and it all adds up to conditions vastly more difficult, draining and dangerous than anything the climbers planned for.

A Team of Three is particularly inefficient for serious roped climbing. When Kelly, Brian and Jerry were climbing either unroped or moving simultaneously while roped together, the configuration of three was just fine. However, as soon as the hard climbing began, the climbers would have turned to the use of anchors and belaying a lead climber, and sitting.

While the lead climber was making his way up the difficult Couloirs, another man was taking the role of belayer, feeding the rope out as the lead man climbed but ever-prepared to haul in and lock down on the rope should the leader fall. The third climber is doing nothing but sitting and getting cold. Compounding the inefficiency, once the lead climber finishes the pitch, or rope length, and sets an anchor, he must bring not one but two people up from below. You've just wasted time, gotten colder, fallen behind schedule, burned the unforgiving fuel called 'time' on your way to the summit of Mount Hood.

The Snow Platform, which was throughout the incident referred to as the "First Snow Cave" by the media suggests both timing and event clues. Recall that the media coverage on December 17th was about the "snow cave" with the strange "Y" of rope outside of it. With the scrutiny of the climbing rescuers, it turns out, the "snow cave" was actually a well-built "snow platform."

The difference is simple - you may spend the night inside a "snow cave" which must be deep enough to provide virtually complete protection from the wind. However, a night at 11,000 feet on Mount Hood on a snow platform is not survivable. A snow platform is not much more than a notch cut into the side of the mountain giving a tiny bit of level ground.

The architecture of this "snow platform" provided only partial protection from the wind, it was embellished on to have deeper side walls. This could spare the body core from the direct wind. Typically, the primary purpose of a snow platform is as a belay stop. Climbers might embellish the snow platform to be able to sit and have a meal or short rest. There will be some kind of anchors used, and the climbers will be directly clipped into this. The size and level of embellishment of the snow platform indicated how much time the climbers spent there.

It is larger than a quick stop. Walls suggesting the need to find some brief respite from the elements. A place, perhaps, to bring the team back into a semblance of equilibrium. This is the clue that something other than normal took place in this are of the climb. It might have been simple exhaustion. It might have been a fall which was not catastrophic to the entire team as a unit, but debilitating to one or more climbers. If one man were injured the fact of having two others would now be a strength.

The Rescue Bind occurred on Saturday, December 9th when the three men were holed up in the snow cave about 300 feet below the summit on the East Face. There, with Kelly unable to go further, they must have had the discussion about who, if anyone, would go for rescue. Should one man go alone for rescue? Should the two able-bodied climbers, Brian and Jerry both go? Should the three men stay together in the snow cave and wait for rescue? Evidence suggests that they decided to send the two men for rescue - Kelly James remaining alone in the snow cave. Certainly the decision was unanimous, as the spirit of the climbing brotherhood dictates.

However, and this is speculative, a reading of each man's climbing history tea-leaves which portends the roles they appear to have ultimately taken. Kelly James, as the reader may remember, had survived four days in a snow cave on Mount McKinley - he could count on that experience to hang on for a couple of days on Mount Hood in a snow cave. Jerry "Nikko" Cooke had been a true rescue hero by holding his climbing partner who had fallen into a crevasse on Mount Rainier. These prior experiences might have weighed the decision to go for rescue higher than the hole-it-out strategy.

Being from Out-of-state and on a Short Time Schedule, it was all on a schedule, every piece of their modern lives. The men's lives were incredibly busy with careers, families and friends. Precious few days could be taken for such idle play as darting off to climb a mountain. But Mount Hood was on the schedule. There were airline reservations, a rental car, only a long weekend to climb a big volcanic mountain in winter.

The local weather forecast showed a low-level front approaching - but it just so happened that if they climbed fast enough they might beat it. As men who had been on other big mountains, they must have checked a local forecast once in Oregon but believed their plan would get them up and down the mountain before the weather caved in. That was probably taken into consideration, but they bet that they could beat the weather with speed, at the same time they compromised on survival gear.

Going Fast and Light on Gear, food and water, the balance is between speed of ascent and the weight of gear brought along. Carry more gear and you will move more slowly but you will have more resources on hand. If you adopt the strategy of going fast, then you must accept the corollary of going lite. So our climbers each brought with them the gear they thought would work during a fast ascent of Mount Hood in early December 2006.

That meant a combination of having bivy sacks and sleeping bags or enough warm cloths to essentially act as a sleeping bag in the bivy sack. There was no tent - and a tent certainly would not have helped in the weather encountered so high on Mount Hood. That was a good decision. To this day we do not have a complete equipment list. How many small shovels did they have along? This would be a factor in their ability to dig snow caves. Ice axes help, but a shovel or shovels would have been required up there.

They probably had a stove and about a day's worth of fuel along with them on the North Face climb. If so, it most likely would have been used late on Friday night after reaching the summit and on Saturday while all three men stayed part of the day together in the snow cave. No stove was found with Kelly James. Brian and Jerry must have taken it or it was discarded as useless without any more fuel. There was a gallon of fuel left in the car.

While they had a working stove with them on the climb they could have melted snow for more water and increased the air temperature in the snow cave. Once the fuel was used up dehydration would not be long behind.

In this scenario, where they have a stove, the hypothermic climbers build a snow cave during darkness on Friday night, having come down from the summit, and are at the limits of their endurance and dangerously hypothermic. Yet, with a stove turned on the temperature in the snow cave would quickly rise, their hands and feet could gently be rewarmed. Room temperature could go into the 30s or higher. Snow could be heated and hot drinks delivered. This quickly helps turn around the course of dehydration and helps with reheating from the inside via the hot drinks. Using a stove in the snow cave might have allowed the men to recover better than they were able to without a stove.

Navigation and Avalanche Gear, from what is known the men had none of the sophisticated equipment. No Global Positioning System ever kicked in. The one piece of technology was the cell phone, which worked once, for four minutes, but was enough to kick off the search while Kelly James was alive. The Mountain Locator Device is a short wave signaler which can be picked up with portable tracking devices. In an accident only two months later, the injured party was found using a Mountain Locator Device.

Speed of Elevation Gain was a factor shadowing the climbers on their journey from comfortable lives in low-lying cities to the summit of Mount Hood at 11,240 feet above sea level. Kelly and Brian were residents of the Dallas, Texas, area - elevation 430 feet above sea level. Jerry Cooke was from New York City - elevation 33 feet above sea level. Two days before the men left a note at their rental car near the base of Mount Hood, they were at homes in their respective cities - living not far above sea level.

Assuming they flew into Portland, Oregon, on Wednesday, December 6th, 2006, we may tag their elevation as 50 feet above sea level. No acclimatization on Wednesday. By the next day they had driven up to the north side of Mount Hood. Parking at the trailhead approximately 3,937 feet above sea level, they hiked the 2.7 miles and 1,900 foot of elevation gain along the Tilly Jane Ski Trail. This is the grand entranceway to the north side of the mountain. In summer there is a way to drive to the Tilly Jane Recreation Area where the men were headed. But in winter all access is by the scenic trail.

The Tilly Jane Recreation Area is bustling in summer, where it has long been a mountain retreat. In winter only the hardy visit. Those who want to go into the back country. Among those with the spirit to challenge winter were Kelly, Brian and Jerry.

Deviation from Plan, interestingly, in the note they left at the Tilly Jane warming hut it mentioned that they were not originally planning to spend the night at the hut, but that the warm fire enticed them to spend the night. What was the original plan? The idea in the heads of the climbers upon leaving their car that morning was to make it up to the Tilly Jane Recreation Area, a walk of only 2.7 miles with a modest elevation gain of 1,900 feet, take a nice break, and then head back out and up the hill. At the Tilly Jane warming hut you are at 5,837 feet above sea level, a full **5,403** vertical feet from the 11,240 summit of Mount Hood.

In the original plan the climbers would make a short stop at Tilly Jane warming hut and continue up to as close to the serious North Face climbing as they could get. Every foot in elevation they knocked off on Thursday would be one less on Friday - the day of the summit bid. If they had been able to gain another 1,000 feet of vertical height, that would leave the summit bid at **4,403 feet** further.

Ideally, the climbers would hike in on Thursday for another 2,000 feet of elevation beyond the Tilly Jane warming hut and get to within a few hundred yards of the start of the actual roped climbing. If this had been executed, the distance to the summit would have been reduced to about **3,403 feet**, something that could be accomplished in a strong morning effort next day. Then you would summit at noon and have all afternoon to get as far back down the mountain as possible in daylight.

One can sympathize with the climbers decision to spend the night in the hut. The alternative to the warm Tilly Jane was going to be a brisk snow cave at 8,000 feet. Unfortunately, the effects of this seemingly small deviation from the plan were huge, catastrophic really. It all of a sudden changed the summit day requirement from 3,403 feet of vertical gain to being 5,403 feet of vertical gain in one short day of climbing, and then having to descend to a survivable level, say another 2,000 or 3,000 feet. Not only did the amount of vertical climb increase greatly by this decision to spend the night, but even more costly was the time factor. By spending the night at Tilly Jane warming hut, they were giving up precious hours of the next morning. Pushing all events at least 1/3 to ½ of a day further back, they could not possibly be on the summit by noon. The afternoon that was potentially open for the descent was being spent in the summit bid.

This cozy night in the hut was silently, insidiously, stacking up long odds against the climbers. Knowing the bonds between climbers, one suspects it may also have been one of the happiest nights the men ever had as climbers.

Dehydration is a constant nemesis in winter. Exertion, perspiration, respiration all drain the average level of hydration. If the climber is not replacing this in quantity a deficit quickly builds up. In winter the added problem of having to melt snow after the provisions brought are used up. The climbers probably had a stove with them but only enough fuel for one night. They left a gallon of fuel in the car. They might have been able to melt snow Friday night but would have run out by sometime on Saturday. No fuel and no running stove by Sunday.

Location of the Snow Cave on the East Face of Mount Hood, not the North Face, clarifies the climber's intent. On the platform they initiated the "bail" plan, good climbers have them, to reach the summit area and immediately descent via a reversal of the Cooper Spur Route, through some tricky rock channels, down to the relatively gentle Cooper Spur and escape. However, they must have reached the summit area in darkness and white-out conditions. In the relatively small confines of a summit, as dictated by mathematics, even a few yards difference can send a climber down the completely wrong face. The Cooper Spur was a sharp left. Literally just yards from where topping out then head down. Taking just a bit softer left-hand turn, easy to understand in the blinding conditions they must surely have been in, sent them past the Cooper Spur descent onto the deeply channeled, rock-outcropping laced, plainly evil East Face with feature names such as Devil's Kitchen and the Black Spider. They did not know this when they built their snow cave - they were hoping it was somewhere on the Cooper Spur. Having correctly identified the location of the snow cave greatly increases the chances of finding Brian and Jerry.

In conclusion, far from having all the stars align in their winter bid for the North Face of Mount Hood, Kelly, Brian and Jerry allowed a cascade of smaller errors to compound until at the end they were over-taken and never released from the icy grip of The Deep Blue Zone on Mount Hood.

The Final Class Act

(Sometime between December 10th and 11th, 2006)

When searchers found the lifeless body of climber Kelly James, late in the day on December 17th, it shattered what for many Americans was the hoped for Christmas miracle of 2006. The country needed a good news story, and for a long week in December this had been the hope - that three brave climbers would somehow come off that wintery mountain alive. That against all odds, these men, who as the story came out were apparently decent and noble individuals, would beat those odds and make it home.

Sure, there was debate over the costs of the rescue operation, the risks people took in search of the men. And citizens, most of them non-climbers, debated the very premise of winter climbing. Non-climbers argued about how selfish it was for the three men to go off and climb what looked like an absurd project. But these men had no death wish. Indeed, there are indications that this group was working their way up to an attempt on Mount Everest.

But among climbers we understood that it was a carefully weighed set of risks they balanced when they made their decision. And they had every belief and every intention of climbing that mountain and coming back home in one piece to the people they loved and cared for most.

No doubt the Mount Hood project was a test for these three men. A test unanimously agreed upon. With a plan that was pushing the envelope. The lighting fast ascent of Mount Hood was a risky but elegant climbing plan. The measure for error was slim. Without question they underestimated early winter on Mount Hood , and how quickly the Deep Blue Zone could appear and engulf. Without doubt they lacked sufficient gear to survive long in the Deep Blue Zone.

But it could have worked! If only... If only they had simply picnicked at the Tilly Jane warming hut and then continued up the mountain to as high as they could go that first Thursday. Somewhere near the start of the serious climbing, they would have dug a snow cave and spent the night. If the night had been too much for them, perhaps they would have backed off on Friday morning. Or, from that starting point, with only 2,500 feet of vertical climbing to gain, they would have flashed the couloirs and hit the summit by late morning. Then all afternoon, for 4-5 hours would have been available for them to high-tail it down. Having balanced the two days - Kelly James would have been stronger in this execution of the climbing plan.

But as it happened that one seemingly small change, which brought with it dreadful imbalances for the climbers, was the path taken. They were good men on a good climb, climbing well but on a fatal trajectory.

The coroner found no disabling injury on the body of climber Kelly James although abrasion on his legs suggested that he had been involved in a fall. The cause of death was ruled to be hypothermia with dehydration a contributing factor. He probably died not long after his call on December 10th, the week before being discovered in the snow cave.

In all likelihood, Kelly had not lasted long after that cell phone call to his family back in Texas. He was wearing Long Johns (top and bottom), light sweater, Gortex jacket, Gortex Ski pants, mittens and double plastic boots for warmth. For climbing he still had a harness, crampons, helmet, four carabiners. The 18 inch ice hammer with him was owned by Jerry. No sleeping bag, no bivy sack, he was laying on his empty pack.

As victims of hypothermia drift off into a dreamy delusional world; when the temperature of the limbs has gone low, but the core gets warmer, just before all heat is lost, men have been known to undress themselves because they feel this phantom heat, the last remaining flicker of their existence.

We know Kelly James did not succumb to this. He was found fully clothed, lying on his side on top of his pack, without a bivy sack covering, a peaceful not grimaced look on his face. He was a devoutly religious man and would have been surrendering himself to the Almighty. But there at the last ebb of Kelly James' existence came one last effort of his love and humanity.

When the rescue climbers who first entered the snow cave saw a body, they did not know who it was. One oddity quickly caught their attention. The victim had intentionally taken off his right hand glove, and curled back all his fingers except his ring finger which at first looked to the rescuers like they were being flipped the 'bird' until they examined closely. On the finger was a class ring, and the telling initials of its owner. Family members confirmed it was Kelly James that night.

The very last gesture of this passing climber was an expression of love to his family, that he definitely be identified, so that there would be no uncertainty as to his fate on Mount Hood that December in 2006. Sadly, that same level of closure has not been afforded to the families of Brian and Jerry because, as of the First Edition of this book, their bodies had not yet been recovered from under the winter snows of Mount Hood. But when they are, as nature releases the secrets of those last fatal moments, it will be the final act in this tragic encounter between three climbers and The Deep Blue Zone.

Search and Recovery

By the summer of 2007 the bodies of Brian Hall and Jerry "Nikko" Cooke have not yet been found or recovered. But that does not mean they are abandoned. Family, friends, and many of the professional and volunteer folks who worked tirelessly at the original December 2006 incident continued their efforts in calm, logical fashion. In February the base of the North Face was searched, and areas lower, including the Tilly Jane hut - where poling through deep snow hit a board hiding the climber's cache, leaving this a secret until a July 2007 search found the items. In August 2007, four friends of climber Brian Hall searched the logical catchment area which may hold their friend and this will be repeated in September by a large-scale search. Where is the highest probability search area for Brian and Nikko? It is not below the North Face, on the Eliot Glacier, as the media and cultural myth has placed them - but around the corner, on the East Face with the Newton Clark Glacier below.

Annotated summer photo of Mount Hood (Photo Credit: Author)

Table W1:   Weather Conditions on Mount Hood for climber's hike from the Snow Park (@3,937' elevation) up to the Tilly Jane warming hut (@5,837' elevation) and remainder of the day spent there.

Tilly Jane warming hut -Thursday, December 7th, 2006

Day	Hour (PST)	Temp (F)	Wind Ave/Max (mph)	Wind Dir.	Precip. liquid (in.)	Wind Chill (F)	Climbers. (Estimated) Elevation, ft.
Dec 7	000	37°	8/12	268	0	31°	<3,000
Dec 7	100	38°	9/18	273	0	32°	<3,000
Dec 7	200	35°	10/16	271	0	27°	<3,000
Dec 7	300	33°	12/18	269	0	24°	<3,000
Dec 7	400	34°	13/20	262	0	25°	<3,000
Dec 7	500	33°	11/19	266	0	24°	<3,000
Dec 7	600	33°	10/15	276	0	25°	<3,000
Dec 7	700	33°	10/15	275	0	25°	<3,000
Dec 7	800	34°	10/15	273	0	26°	3,937
Dec 7	900	37°	10/17	260	0	30°	(4,570)
Dec 7	1000	39°	12/20	262	0	32°	(5,203)
Dec 7	1100	40°	12/20	264	0	33°	5,837
Dec 7	1200	42°	12/21	267	0	35°	5,837
Dec 7	1300	47°	11/21	265	0	42°	5,837
Dec 7	1400	45°	11/21	276	0	39°	5,837
Dec 7	1500	46°	13/22	279	0	40°	5,837
Dec 7	1600	43°	13/23	276	0	36°	5,837
Dec 7	1700	39°	15/24	269	0	31°	5,837
Dec 7	1800	38°	14/22	264	0	30°	5,837
Dec 7	1900	37°	10/19	269	0	30°	5,837
Dec 7	2000	38°	9/19	262	0	32	5,837
Dec 7	2100	38°	10/15	256	0	31°	5,837
Dec 7	2200	39°	11/19	264	0	32°	5,837
Dec 7	2300	36°	15/22	262	0	27°	5,837

Version 1 to Feb. 19, 2007. Use with Permission of the Author only.

* Note: Proxy values of temperature and precipitation. from 5,250', wind values from 6,600'.

Table W2:   Estimated Weather Conditions on Mount Hood for climber's at elevation-appropriate levels on the summit day, beginning at the Tilly Jane warming hut.

Summit Day - Friday, December 8th, 2006

Day	Hour (PST)	Temp (F)	Wind Ave/Max (mph)	Wind Dir.	Precip. Total (in.)	Wind Chill (F)	Climbers. (Estimated) (@5250ft) Elevation, ft.
Dec 8	000	37°	8/15	263	0	31°	5,837
Dec 8	100	37°	6/13	264	0	32°	5,837
Dec 8	200	36°	10/16	264	0	29°	5,837
Dec 8	300	34°	8/15	262	0	27°	5,837
Dec 8	400	34°	6/14	267	0	29°	5,837
Dec 8	500	34°	6/13	271	0	29°	5,837
Dec 8	600	36°	6/15	269	0	31°	5,837
Dec 8	700	36°	1/9	267	0	36°	5,837
Dec 8	800	39°	7/14	263	0	34°	(6,500)
Dec 8	900	42°	13/24	267	0	35°	(7,200)
Dec 8	1000	38°	17/30	55	0	29°	(7,800)
Dec 8	1100	39°	22/38	268	0	29°	(8,500)
Dec 8	1200	31°	28/56	261	0	17°	(9,200)
Dec 8	1300	30°	33/52	266	0	14°	(9,900)
Dec 8	1400	26°	33/51	263	0	9°	(10,500)
Dec 8	1500	24°	38/45	262	0	5°	(11,239)
Dec 8	1600	20°	39/49	262	0	-1°	(11,239)
Dec 8	1700	21°	42/52	267	0	0°	(11,239)
Dec 8	1800	20°	39/53	263	0	-1°	(11,089)
Dec 8	1900	21°	39/51	261	0	1°	10,900
Dec 8	2000	21°	43/58	261	0	0°	10,900
Dec 8	2100	19°	44/57	262	0	-3°	10,900
Dec 8	2200	16°	42/55	252	0	-7°	10,900
Dec 8	2300	17°	40/55	251	0	-5°	10,900

Version 1 to Feb. 1, 2007/Up-dated 2/20/7. Use with Permission of the Author only.

86

Table W3:   Estimated Weather Conditions on Mount Hood for climber's at the approximate elevation of the snow cave, about 11,000 feet on the North Face of Mount Hood.

Saturday, December 9th, 2006

Day	Hour (PST)	Temp (F)	Wind Ave/Max (mph)	Wind Dir.	Precip. liquid (in.)	Wind Chill (F)	Climbers. (Estimated) (@5250ft) Elevation, ft.
Dec 9	000	17°	39/49	243	0	- 5°	10,900
Dec 9	100	16°	38/46	247	0	- 6°	10,900
Dec 9	200	16°	39/49	259	0	- 6°	10,900
Dec 9	300	13°	38/46	256	0	-10°	10,900
Dec 9	400	13°	41/51	257	0.14	-11°	10,900
Dec 9	500	12°	39/47	255	0.10	-12°	10,900
Dec 9	600	13°	42/51	254	0.07	-11°	10,900
Dec 9	700	13°	45/56	257	0.14	-12°	10,900
Dec 9	800	14°	54/71	257	0.06	-12°	10,900
Dec 9	900	15°	58/75	263	0.01	-11°	10,900
Dec 9	1000	15°	55/81	267	0	-11°	10,900
Dec 9	1100	14°	52/75	264	0.01	-12°	10,900
Dec 9	1200	15°	54/78	281	0	-10°	10,900
Dec 9	1300	15°	49/69	281	0	-10°	10,900
Dec 9	1400	15°	45/61	278	0.02	- 9°	10,900
Dec 9	1500	14°	46/58	275	0	-10°	10,900
Dec 9	1600	14°	43/63	279	0	-10°	10,900
Dec 9	1700	13°	41/53	271	0	-11°	10,900
Dec 9	1800	14°	40/49	264	0	-9°	10,900
Dec 9	1900	15°	33/39	208	0	-6°	10,900
Dec 9	2000	15°	36/48	147	0	-7°	10,900
Dec 9	2100	15°	35/47	88	0	-7°	10,900
Dec 9	2200	16°	34/47	127	0	-5°	10,900
Dec 9	2300	16°	32/39	194	0	-5°	10,900

Table W4:   Estimated Weather Conditions on Mount Hood for 11,000 foot elevation on the North Face of Mount Hood.

Cell Phone Call - Sunday, December 10th, 2006

Day	Hour (PST)	Temp (F)	Wind Ave/Max (mph)	Wind Dir.	(@5250ft) Precip. liquid (in.)	Wind Chill (F)	Climbers. (Estimated) Elevation, ft.
Dec 10	000	15°	35/44	216	0	- 7°	10,900
Dec 10	100	15°	35/45	219	0	- 7°	10,900
Dec 10	200	15°	36/16	251	0.03	- 7°	10,900
Dec 10	300	14°	39/49	236	0	- 9°	10,900
Dec 10	400	14°	39/22	242	0	- 9°	10,900
Dec 10	500	14°	40/19	244	0	- 9°	10,900
Dec 10	600	14°	43/52	257	0	-10°	10,900
Dec 10	700	13°	47/55	251	0	-12°	10,900
Dec 10	800	13°	49/59	254	0.01	-12°	10,900
Dec 10	900	12°	50/62	255	0.02	-14°	10,900
Dec 10	1000	11°	51/73	265	0	-16°	10,900
Dec 10	1100	12°	51/75	282	0	-14°	10,900
Dec 10	1200	12°	51/79	275	0	-14°	10,900
Dec 10	1300	12°	52/70	271	0.02	-14°	10,900
Dec 10	1400	12°	53/79	279	0.01	-15°	10,900
Dec 10	1500	11°	54/76	279	0.01	-16°	10,900
Dec 10	1600	11°	59/88	283	0.02	-17°	10,900
Dec 10	1700	11°	61/82	283	0.02	-17°	10,900
Dec 10	1800	9°	66/86	285	0.01	-21°	10,900
Dec 10	1900	10°	58/73	284	0	-18°	10,900
Dec 10	2000	10°	58/78	288	0.01	-18°	10,900
Dec 10	2100	10°	49/69	280	0	-17°	10,900
Dec 10	2200	10°	45/63	277	0.02	-16°	10,900
Dec 10	2300	10°	46/59	279	0	-16°	10,900

Table W5:   Estimated Weather Conditions on Mount Hood for 11,000 foot elevation on the North Face of Mount Hood.

First Search Day - Monday, December 11, 2006

Day	Hour (PST)	Temp (F)	Wind Ave/Max (mph)	Wind Dir.	Precip. liquid (in.)	Wind Chill (F)	Climbers. (Estimated) Elevation, ft.
					(@5250ft)		
Dec 11	000	10°	49/64	280	0	-17°	10,900
Dec 11	100	11°	46/60	276	0	-15°	10,900
Dec 11	200	13°	48/62	263	0.03	-12°	10,900
Dec 11	300	14°	51/71	257	0.07	-11°	10,900
Dec 11	400	14°	51/64	261	0.03	-11°	10,900
Dec 11	500	15°	49/64	262	0	-10°	10,900
Dec 11	600	15°	48/60	259	0	- 9°	10,900
Dec 11	700	15°	47/60	260	0	- 9°	10,900
Dec 11	800	15°	50/69	257	0.01	-10°	10,900
Dec 11	900	15°	52/66	256	0.05	-10°	10,900
Dec 11	1000	16°	52/64	256	0	- 9°	10,900
Dec 11	1100	16°	60/75	252	0.07	-10°	10,900
Dec 11	1200	16°	64/77	251	0.05	-11°	10,900
Dec 11	1300	17°	66/88	253	0.10	- 9°	10,900
Dec 11	1400	17°	62/81	258	0.13	- 9°	10,900
Dec 11	1500	17°	52/76	273	0.20	- 7°	10,900
Dec 11	1600	16°	60/87	267	0.10	-10°	10,900
Dec 11	1700	14°	60/87	257	0.09	-13°	10,900
Dec 11	1800	14°	64/93	253	0.04	-13°	10,900
Dec 11	1900	12°	61/92	267	0.09	-16°	10,900
Dec 11	2000	13°	60/96	283	0.02	-14°	10,900
Dec 11	2100	14°	60/86	261	0	-13°	10,900
Dec 11	2200	14°	63/83	256	0	-13°	10,900
Dec 11	2300	15°	64/85	256	0.04	-12°	10,900

Summary of Cable News Network (CNN) Coverage of the Mount Hood Climbing Accident, December 11 - 20, 2006.

	Days Run	Lead Story	Total Segments	Mt. Hood Segments	Percent Mt. Hood	First Run	Last Run
CNN Newsroom	9	3	208	32	15.38 %	11th	20th
Anderson Cooper 360°	7	3	71	10	14.08 %	12th	20th
American Morning	5	2	61	13	21.31 %	14th	20th
Paula Zahn Now	2	0	5	2	40.00 %	14th	18th
CNN Saturday Morning	1	1	6	1	16.67 %	16th	16th
CNN Sunday Morning	1	0	4	1	25.00 %	17th	17th
The Situation Room	3	1	31	6	19.35 %	18th	20th
		10	386	65	16.84 %		

Source of data:
1. Tracking of the Mount Hood story as covered by CNN was done using their website, www.cnn.com. December 2006.

Show Credits:
1. CNN Newsroom, © 2007 Cable News Network LP, LLLP.
   A Time Warner Company. All Rights Reserved.
2. Anderson Cooper 360°© 2007 Cable News Network LP, LLLP.
   A Time Warner Company. All Rights Reserved.
3. American Morning, © 2007 Cable News Network LP, LLLP.
   A Time Warner Company. All Rights Reserved.
4. Paula Zahn Now, © 2007 Cable News Network LP, LLLP.
   A Time Warner Company. All Rights Reserved.
5. CNN Saturday Morning,© 2007 Cable News Network LP, LLLP.
   A Time Warner Company. All Rights Reserved.
6. CNN Sunday Morning,© 2007 Cable News Network LP, LLLP.
   A Time Warner Company. All Rights Reserved.
7. The Situation Room, © 2007 Cable News Network LP, LLLP.
   A Time Warner Company. All Rights Reserved.

Table use with Permission of the Author only.

Biographies

Kelly James:
Dallas Texas
Age:48
Wife: Karen
Children: Jason, Ford, Katie, and Jack
Mother: Lou Ann Cameron
Siblings: Youngest of four brothers, Frank James
        Ben James and sister Traci Hale
Profession: Landscape Architect since 1989
Grew up in a Dallas Texas suburb.
School: Texas Tech University of Lubbock
Studied: Agronomy
Climbing for 25 years.
Climbs: Alps, Andes, Matterhorn, Mt Aconcagua (highest mountain in South America) and Mount Rainier.
Survived a four day blizzard while on Mount McKinley.

Brian Hall:
Dallas Texas
Age:37
Father: Dwight Hall
Born in Germany, raised in South Dakota
Profession: Personal Trainer
School: Central City High School in Rapid City, South Dakota
Degree in business management on a scholarship from University of Connecticut where he was the goalie for the Huskies soccer team in the late 1980s and a walk-on to the basketball team. In 1986 he was a runner up for South Dakota's Mr. Basketball Award. He was described by friends as being a "Gentle Hercules" with the spirit of Peter Pan who rescued strays, helped the homeless and was a mentor to young soccer players. He often volunteered and raised money for charities like Habitat for Humanity. This climb was a practice run for Mount Everest.

Jerry "Nikko" Cooke:
Brooklyn, New York
Age: 36
Wife: Michaela Javan
Mother: Maria Kim - A first generation Korean immigrant.
Profession: Attorney for Countrywide Insurance - cars
Grew up in New York's Chinatown in a basement apartment.
School: State University of New York at Stonybrook in late 1980s.
Climbs: Sulphide Glacier on Washington's Mount Shuksan, Mount Rainier.
July 2005 while climbing Emmons Glacier on the face of Washington's Mount Rainier with David Valdes. Cooke was trailing and Valdes was on a harness rope when he fell ten feet through a cravasse, he then fell another ten feet. Cooke kept his footing and stopped the fall. They were helped by two other climbers.
He met Kelly and Brian while climbing Mount Rainier.
Friends say he was a natural survivor with tremendous work ethics.
His credo: "You can do anything you want to but just make sure you are back in time for work."
He was fond of saying "The world is in front of you."

Notes

Weather Estimates:

Weather estimates used in this book, for the time the climbers spent at or above 11,000 feet, were made using the following methodology. The author used raw data from the Mount Hood, Meadows Ski Area weather stations, maintained by the Northwest Weather and Avalanche Center as the raw data. There were some variables collected at 5,250 feet and others at 6,600 feet above sea level and data at both levels were used. For every 1,000 feet of elevation gain, temperature was reduced by 3.7° F. with starting values from the 6600 foot level.

Wind is more difficult to estimate. While tracking this story in the media, meteorologists were providing a correction factor of adding 30mph to basis wind values at 6600 feet up to the 11,000 foot level at least for gusts. The author spoke with Kenny Kramer, Ph.D. an avalanche meteorologist at the Northwest Weather and Avalanche Center, who cautioned me about the micro-effects and the uncertainty in making wind estimates for the summit area. I was chastened. It was clearly okay to add that 30mph for basis winds 20mph, 30, mph, 40 mph at the height of a big mountain in winter. But was a fudge-factor of 30mph appropriate to adjust winds of only 10mph?

Electronically visiting the Mount Washington, New Hampshire, weather station site found a dataset to at least 'reality check' the use of 30mph as the correction factor used throughout this book. Each day the forecast for the high summits and the Mount Washington Valley are posted. Just a small sampling of days in January, 2007 shows that the difference between lower and the very highest elevations can be substantial, even when not extraordinary.

The Mount Washington data shows, even at a week's glance, that the difference between winds in the valley and wind speeds on the high summits of the Presidential Range are substantial, here ranging from a difference of 10 mph to 60mph. Based on this small study, the author suggests that a fudge factor of 30mph on Mount Hood is probably reasonable, if not conservative, especially in storm.

Table W6: Wind data from the Mount Washington Observatory comparing the High Summits to the Mount Washington Valley, January 2007.

Date 2007	Summit Day	Valley Day	Diff. Range	Summit Night	Valley Night	Diff. Range
Jan 11	35-50	10	25-40	55-75	10-15	40-60
Jan 12	60-75	10-15	45-60	55-70	10	45-60
Jan 13	40-60	10	30-50	20-35	10	10-25
Jan 15	35-50	8	27-42	20-40	8	12-32
Jan 15	40-50	10	30-40	40-60	10	30-40
Jan 16	50-70	10-15	35-55	50-70	10-15	35-55
Jan 17	65-90	10-15	50-75	25-60	5	20-55

* All wind values and differences are in miles per hour (mph).
Source: www.mountwashington.org/weather, Jan. 2007.

Estimating the climber's weather on December 8th, the day of the climb from the Tilly Jane ski hut to summit and the bivouac in first snow cave, involved a simplified assumption about their movement that day, and the temperature and wind adjustments required to correct for the climber's progress up the mountain. Assuming they began at 7am and reached the summit at 3pm. Divide the elevation and get an average of 675.25 feet per hour. In reality the later part of the climbing, roped up the couloirs, would have been far slower than the pace at the start. Nonetheless, using this average value, 675.25 feet per hour, the author estimated the teams elevation at each hour, then corrected the raw weather data, using straight-line extrapolation for both temperature and wind, to make estimates hour by hour.

December 7th was the day the climbers hiked up to the Tilly Jane warming hut. Weather values from the Meadows Stations at 5,250 feet and 6,600 feet are used without any adjustment.

Glossary

Alpine style climbing - Traveling light and fast. Acclimation and fitness are key to success in this form of travel.

Altitude sickness - Also known as High Altitude Pulmonary Edema. The alveolar/capillary membrane leaks fluid into the air sacs of the lungs, possibly causing the victim to drown.

Avalanche danger Scale - The United States Avalanche Danger Scale was revised in 1996 and has five levels: Low, Moderate, Moderate to High, High and Extreme. At the upper end either human or natural caused avalanches are likely.

Belay - Climbing technique to protect a leader from a long fall.

Bivouac - A crude overnight encampment.

Bivouac sack - Used in place of a tent for temporary shelter when traveling light.

Blizzard - Wintery conditions including high winds (typically 35mph or greater), cold and visibility limited by falling snow and/or wind-driven existing snows for at least three hours. There is no specific temperature requirement. No new snow has to fall in a blizzard, as long as a snow base is stirred up to reduce visibility, down to within one-quarter of a mile, often much less.

Climbing anchor - One or more pieces of equipment to support belay or top-rope weight.

Cornice - A formation of ice and snow which overhangs from the summit edge over steep walls like the North Face of Mount Hood.

Couloir - A deep mountainside gully or gorge usually containing snow or ice.

Crampons - Metal spikes strapped onto mountain boots, typically ten points with two fang-like front points (12-point crampons).

Deep Blue Zone - A non-technical term coined by the author. Conditions of high average wind speeds (25mph-30mph or greater) and temperatures leading to a Wind Chill Factor of zero degrees Fahrenheit or below. On a mountain with an existing snow base, these high winds, even without new snow, will create white-out conditions, increase avalanche danger, and quickly drain a climber exposed to the elements.

Drone - Unmanned aerial plane with information gathering capabilities such as photographic imagery and or heat-seeking capability. Typically a miniature aircraft controlled by computer.

Frostbite - An injury due to exposure to cold, usually limited to areas that do not contain large muscles for heat generation and are not vital for survival, thus are the first place for blood flow reduction. This only occurs when temperatures are below freezing. Severity depends on amount of exposure time. Acclimation decreases susceptibility. High altitude also has its effects as there is increased hypoxia thus decreasing resistance to cold injuries. Injury is usually by dehydration due to the extraction of fluid from the cells forming ice crystals in the tissues. Blood flow is also impaired "starving" the effected tissue.

Hasty Team - The first Search and Rescue team up the mountain. The hasty team quickly searches the most likely places the search object was last seen or active in.

Hypothermia - Cooling of the entire bode to below the level needed for normal body function. Hypothermia has three stages, the first being mild to strong shivering when the body temperatures drop as low as 95°F (35°C), goose bumps rise to attempt insulation and the hands become numb. The second stage is where shivering becomes more violent, as the core temperature drops to as low as 91°F (33°C). The victim becomes cyanotic and pale. Movement is difficult and uncoordinated, the victim is often confused at this point. When the core temperature drops to 90°F (32°C) shivering stops, gross body movements (arms and legs) are difficult, fine motor skills (fingers) are almost impossible. The victim becomes irrational and often suffers from dysrhythmias and organ failure. Death follows.

Hypoxia - Lowered oxygen level in the blood. (Sometime referred to as hypoxemia)

Ice Axe - The most versatile piece of equipment for snow and ice travel, it helps balance the climber, provides points of security to prevent falls or to arrest a fall. Different sizes have different uses.

Ice screws - Tubular aluminum 3" to 12" with threads and sharp edges at one end and an eye at the other end which can be screwed into ice for protection.. Often used for an anchor.

Metabolism - The energy derived from food processed by the body and measured in Calories. The glucose stored in muscles is only adequate for a few hours of exercise, then must be replaced with more Calories and oxygen. Body fat is not metabolized fast enough to be useful..

Rack - A sturdy shoulder strap with protective gear clipped onto it such that pieces can be easily pulled off for use as protection while lead climbing.

Running belay - Rather than having one climber anchored while the other leads out, a running belay has both climbers moving at once. The lead climber puts protection in, on the go, building several, hopefully, secure points in case either falls.

Self-Arrest - Use of an ice axe in arrest position to stop a fall down a snow slope.

Snow Picket - Light weight T-bars used to increase holding in soft snow.

Webbing - Climbing webbing is made of ultra strong synthetic material in either flat or tubular form, typically capable of holding over 1,000 lbs of force. Used to link climbing gear while lead climbing and at anchor spots.

Wind Chill Factor - The combined effect of temperature and wind felt on the skin causing body temperature to be lower than in ambient air conditions.

Wind Force - Doubling wind speed from 20 mph to 40 mph creates a wind force more than double - wind force increases geometrically.

Bibliography

Chapter 2: The Climbing Plan
1. Kearney, Alan. Classic Climbs of the Northwest. Alpen Books Press. Washington. 2002. Pages 265-269.

Chapter 3: Tilly Jane Warming Hut
1. Location of the Cooper Spur Shelter, Mount Hood Wilderness Map, Geo-Graphics, Beaverton, Oregon.
2. Surface Weather map for 12/7/2006, National Oceanic and Atmospheric Administrative, www.hpc.ncep.noaa.gov/html/sfc_archive.shtml.

Chapter 6: The Snow Cave
1. Story of Jerry Cooke as rescuer from, "Mt. Hood, Free Our Sons" by Eric Lenkowitz, www.nypost.com, 12/17/2006.

Chapter 7: Alone
1. Kelly James' climb of Mount McKinley, www.oregonlive.com, 12/17/2006

Chapter 8: Search and Rescue
1. KGW tv exclusive interview "One-on-one interview with Sheriff Wampler" Copyright KGW tv, December 20, 2006. www.kgw.com. Transcript by the author. (Permission Pending)
3. Details of first Reports, www.oregonlive.com, 12/11/2006.
4. First national reporting on CNN - Newsroom, from transcript on CNN.com for 12/11/2006.
5. Sunset time in Portland, Oregon from www.timeanddate.com
6. Details of the days search from www.kgw.com on 12/12/2006
7. Quote from Bernie Wells for 12/13, www.oregonlive.com, 12/18/2006.

8. Surface Weather map for 12/13/2006, National Oceanic and Atmospheric Administrative, www.hpc.ncep.noaa.gov/html/sfc_archive.shtml.
9. Reference to the Northwest Weather and Avalanche Center, www.oregonlive.com, 12/18/2006.
10. Quote from Capt. Chris Bernard, www.oregonlive.com, 12/18/2006
11. Details of number of searchers, www.oregonlive.com, 12/15/2006.
12. Details of number of searchers, www.oregonlive.com, 12/17/2006.
13.Family spokeswoman name, www.greatfallstribune.com, 12/18/2006.
14. Detail of 1pm discovery of a snow cave, www.dallasnews.com, 12/18/2006.

Chapter 9: The Media
1. First national reporting on CNN - Newsroom, from transcript on CNN.com for 12/11/2006.

Chapter 10: A Short History of Mount Hood Accidents
1. The 1986 Mount Hood accident from Accidents In North American Mountaineering, The American Alpine Club, 1987.

Chapter 11: Analysis
1. Jim Whittaker quotation from an interview with correspondent by Jerry Bowen, CBS News, 2006, www.cbsnews.com/stories/2006/12/18/national/ main2274929.shtml
2. Mountain Weather Forecast For The Olympics, Washington Cascades and Mt Hood Area, from the Northwest Weather and Avalanche Center, Seattle Washington. 12/6/2006 and 12/7/2006.
3. Story of Jerry Cooke as rescuer from, "Mt. Hood, Free Our Sons" by Eric Lenkowitz, www.nypost.com, 12/17/2006.

Biographies
1. Family information on Kelly James. "Hope, faith sustain kin of 3 missing climbers." by Sandra Pedicini. Orlando Sentinel. www.orlandosentinel.com, 12/14/2007.

Weather Data and Conversions
1. Weather data from Mount Hood, Meadows Ski Area from USDA Forest Service, Northwest Weather and Avalanche Center, www.nwac/us, 12/2006.
2. Wind Chill Calculation: NOAA, National Weather Service, Office of Climate, Water and Weather Services, www.weather.gov/os/windchill/index.shtml. Jan 12/2007.

Glossary
1. United States Avalanche Danger Scale from Northwest Weather and Avalanche Center. www.nwac.us/education_resources/ dangerscale. 2007.

Photo and Illustration Credits

Book Jacket design by Sunflower Vicky Elliott, Hubert A. Allen, Jr., Teresa Bennett.

1. Mount Hood, Front Cover, by the Author, taken 2-2-2007, 4:05pm. (With design added by Sunflower Vicky Elliott).
2. Map of The Western United States of America, graphic by Teresa Bennett, Hubert A. Allen, Jr.
3. Mount Hood, North Face Route, by the Author, taken 2-2-2007, 4:06pm.
4. Tilly Jane warming Hut, by the Author, taken: 2-03-2007, 11:03am.
5. Weather Maps pages 17 and 43 by NOAA
6.. Stove at the Tilly Jane warming Hut, by the Author, taken: 2-03-2007.
7. Register and pay box at the Tilly Jane warming Hut, by the Author, taken: 2-03-2007.
8. Relative location of snow cave, snow cave insert, by the 939th Air Refueling Wing. Courtesy of the Public Affairs Office.
9. Sheriff Joe Wampler, by the 939th Air Refueling Wing. Courtesy of the Public Affairs Office.
10. Searchers in blizzard conditions, by Todd Wells, taken: 12-11-2006, 11:15am. Ref:: Todd_Wells_0001. With Permission of the 304th Rescue Squadron.
11. Black Hawk helicopter last flight on 12/16, by Faith Cathcart, taken: 12-16-2006, 4:27pm. With permission of The Oregonian.
12. Snow Platform, by Todd Wells, taken: 12-17-2006, 2:46pm. Ref: Todd Wells-74. With Permission of the 304th Rescue Squadron.
13. The "Y" shaped climbing anchor, taken 12-18-2006, by the 939th Air Refueling Wing. Courtesy of the Public Affairs Office.

14. Footsteps leading to the summit from the snow platform, taken 12-18-2006. by the 939th Air Refueling Wing. Courtesy of the Public Affairs Office.
15. Snow Cave, by Todd Wells, taken: 12-18-2006, 1:20pm. Ref: Todd Wells-15. With Permission of the 304th Rescue Squadron.
16. The Media, taken 12-19-2006, by the 939th Air Refueling Wing. Courtesy of the Public Affairs Office.
17. The news segue between outdoor sagas December 10-12, 2006, graphic by the Author.
18. Final news segue between outdoor sagas December, graphic by the Author.
19. East Face by the Author.
20. Top of the Mountain, taken: 12-17-2006. With Permission of the 304th Rescue Squadron.

Book Back Cover Photo Montage of five Images:
1. Tilly Jane Hut, by the Author, taken: 2-03-2007, 11:03am.
2. Tilly Jane trailhead, by Jon Williams, taken: 2-03-2007, 9am.
3. Snow Cave, by Todd Wells, taken: 12-18-2006, 1:20pm. Ref: Todd Wells-15. With Permission of the 304th Rescue Squadron. (Upper left photo in montage - printed in mirror image for montage)
4. Search and rescuers near the summit of Mount Hood, by Captain Mark Ross, taken: 12-17-2006. With Permission of the 304th Rescue Squadron.
5. Search and rescuers descend the North Face, by Todd Wells, taken: 12-17-2006, 3:08pm. Ref. Todd_Wells_0076. With Permission of the 304th Rescue Squadron.

If You Go

Be aware that conditions on Mount Hood can change rapidly. A forecast for the Portland area understates conditions high on Mount Hood where climbers are aiming for. Every season has the potential to catch climbers off-guard. When the author climbed here it was summer, on the South Side and the climb was essentially a walk in the park - a beautiful, elegant, fun day on a great mountain. The descent was uneventful. These were the best conditions possible.

But a friend of mine, the distinguished mountaineering book seller Michael Chessler, explained that his South Side summer attempt ended with retreat and him in the early stages of hypothermia. Do not underestimate Mount Hood as our three climbers did. Even the easier routes can become tombs in bad weather for the under-prepared.

If you don't have the gear to survive the bivouac ahead, turn back if things head south (are going bad). Much better to retreat and be able to return another day. How many times did our three climbers consider retreat - and then talk themselves into continuing? We will never know. They were fatally stubborn and clearly should have turned back midway up the North Face. Even as high as the platform, a decisive retreat would have put them at a lower, more survivable elevation.

The best sleeping bag you can afford will come in real handy if that unexpected over night stay out in the elements, in a tent or a snow cave happens. In winter you must bring an exceptionally good sleeping bag in preparation for a night out. A water-proof outer layer is vital to keep the nasty effects of water conducting heat away from the body. Wearing layers is the best form of insulating the body because in the boundary between each successive layer a pocket of dead air effectively traps heat.

Navigation skills and device are essential. At least a compass and the skills to navigate by the compass in a white-out (not many of us can do this - practice in the neighborhood first). The avalanche locator device recently proved helpful in a February 2007 rescue of four climbers and their dog after they fell down a cliff and were benighted.

When asked how they survived the night in the open, on a ledge, they answered with several great suggestions. For one they were positive. They simply talked and supported each other in a positive way. They had cell phone communication with rescuers. They had a routine of being called by the rescuers every hour for a check on how they were doing. They used the group body heat and agility to keep limbs from freezing. Everyone agreed that the dog was a key source of heat, although she was sometimes on top of and sometimes below the people.

They had a locator device and the searchers were able to locate them using the devices tracking system. Still, they had to spend one night out in a dicey position. Rescuers were able to pull them up off the ledge the next day and they walked out.

Build some acclimatization time into your trip to Mount Hood. The summit is 11,239 feet above sea level. Depending on where you are coming from, your hometown elevation, be aware of the potential effects of elevation. Even folks in Portland, 50 feet above sea level, are subject to the biology of altitude physiology. Especially if you do not know the mountain, a day or two spent exploring the slopes and trails is well worth the effort. Knowledge of the local terrain can be priceless.

Foremost, every individual has a unique tolerance for elevation and change in elevation. However, many of us mere mortals are subject to the negative effects. A quick visit to the heights for a couple hours and you can probably get away without major effects. However, if you are benighted, the rules of high altitude physiology get to play out. Headaches, light headedness, deep unproductive breathing and this is mild. Cases of pulmonary edema can occur even at this elevation.

Make sure you have worked your way up the climbing ladder before your Mount Hood summit attempt. Have the technical skills, the survival skills and most importantly have the common sense to list retreat among your options. Stay as far away from the Deep Blue Zone as possible.

Special Thanks

No one was coerced into helping with this project. No one was paid for their time or information by the author. Special thanks are due the following people, in alphabetical order: Allen Family, Susan Allen, Joeff Davis, Muller Davis, Sunflower Elliott, George, Deborah Helitzer, Jon Holleb, Jos, Joel Kinnunen, Drew Klinger, Nyika, Paulene, Steve Rollins, Mark Ross, Sharon and Wayne, David Sklar, Joe Wampler, Jon Williams, Jim Wilson, Gordon and Delia Smith, The Cooper Spur Lodge, Todd Wells and my parents Mary and Hugh Allen. Super special thanks to Teresa Bennett. From the August 2007 research trip thanks to Drew Klinger, Carla and Marin, A, J, S, K.

Other Books Written or Published by Hubert A. Allen, Jr.

The Simpson Incident and Other Climbing Misadventures
Author: Hubert A. Allen, Jr.
Description": 150 pages; Trade Paperback (5.5" by 8.5"),
ISBN: 0-9641694-2-8., 5 B&W photographs, 2 Maps,
Retail US $ 14.95. Copyright 2005 by Hubert A. Allen, Jr.
Published by Hubert Allen and Associates.
Pub. Date: 2008; Street Date: 2005.

Stonehenge Earth and Sky
Authors: Gerald S. Hawkins and Hubert A. Allen, Jr.
Description": 48 pages; UK Trade Paperback (6.6" by 9.7"),
ISBN: 1-903035-24-4.,
29 Color Photographs, 9 B&W Photos, 2 Maps
10 Important Diagrams, including Stonehenge site Maps
Copyright 2003 by Gerald S. Hawkins and Hubert A. Allen, Jr.
Published by Wessex Books, 2004. Pub. Date: 2004.

Christopher Columbus and the Participation of the Jews in the Spanish and Portuguese Discoveries
Author: Meyer Kayserling.
Description": 172 pages; Trade Paperback (5.5 by 8.5"),
ISBN: 0-9641696-9-5.
Retail US $ 19.42. Copyright 2002 by Hubert A. Allen Jr.
Published by Hubert Allen and Associates. Pub. Date 2002.

Beyond Stonehenge
Author: Gerald S. Hawkins
Description": 256 pages; Trade Paperback (7.5" by 8.5"),
ISBN: 0-9641694-8-7.
57&W Photographs, 30 Drawings, including Stonehenge site Maps
Retail US $ 19.95.
Copyright 2001 by Gerald S. Hawkins (original 1973)
Published by Hubert Allen and Associates, 2001. Pub. Date: 2001.

Breakfast with Kamuzu
Author: Hubert A. Allen, Jr., First Edition. Fiction.
Description": 128 pages; Trade Paperback (5.5" by 8.5"),
ISBN: 0-9641694-4-4., 2 Maps
Retail US $ 13.95. Copyright 2001 by Hubert A. Allen, Jr.
Published by Hubert Allen and Associates. Pub. Date: 2001.

The Petroglyph Calendar: An Archaeoastronomy Adventure
Author: Hubert A. Allen, Jr., First Edition.
Description": 152 pages; Trade Paperback (5.5" by 8.5"),
ISBN: 0-9641694-5-2., 3 B&W photographs, 1 Map, 10 Figures
Retail US $ 18.95. Copyright 1998 by Hubert A. Allen, Jr.
Published by Hubert Allen and Associates. Pub. Date: 1998.
Second Edition: 2001

Other Photos

Members of the 304th Pararescue Squadon and the Crag Rats set anchors and ropes for descent onto the North Face, December 17th, 2006. (With Permission of the 304th Rescue Squadron.)

Members of the 304th Pararescue Squadon in the helicopter on December18, 2006. (With Permission of the 304th Rescue Squadron.)

Members of the 304th Pararescue Squadon are briefed by Sheriff Joe Wampler on December 19th, 2006. (With Permission of the 304th Rescue Squadron.)

Black Hawk Helicopter Photo on December 19th, 2006. (With Permission of the 939th Air Refueling Wing.)

Planning Your Trip To Mount Hood
(Just A Reminder)

Team Members:

Climbing Plan:

Plan B:

Departure Date:

Day-by-day descriptions:

Return day:

List of Climbing Gear:

List of food/water:

Navigation tools:

Contact Persons:

And your Reality Check is ????

Best Of Luck!

Hubert A. Allen, Jr. Climber/Author

www.ingramcontent.com/pod-product-compliance
Lightning Source LLC
Chambersburg PA
CBHW060746100426

42813CB00032B/3421/J